T0365825

Spiritual Warfare
The Battle

WRITTEN AND ILLUSTRATED BY:

MADISON MCGARR

AuthorHouse™ LLC
1663 Liberty Drive
Bloomington, IN 47403
www.authorhouse.com
Phone: 1-800-839-8640

Published by AuthorHouse 07/14/2014

ISBN: 978-1-4969-1765-2 (sc)
ISBN: 978-1-4969-1766-9 (e)

authorHOUSE®

CONTENTS

ACKNOWLEDGMENT

"A special thanks to Jerry & Pat Kooi without your help this book would not have been published."

CHAPTER ONE

TRAIN UP A CHILD

My mother made her children spend half of their life in church. Sunday morning was Sunday school for an hour, then preaching for another hour. Sunday evening was Church for an hour and a half. Monday night was C.Y.C., "Christian Youth Crusaders", for two hours, and Wednesday night was Family night for about two hours. In Sunday school, I was taught about Bible heroes like Adam & Eve, Noah's Ark, Joseph and his coat of many colors, David and Goliath, Jonah and the big fish, and many stories about Jesus. Sunday morning church, mom sat in the back pews where we could sleep or do something quietly. Sunday night service mom would do a repeat of Sunday morning church service. Every once in a while, mom would let us skip Sunday night service, and leave us at home with our dad who very seldom went to church with us. We looked forward to Monday night C.Y.C. where we started off with our pledges of allegiance to the Christian and U.S.A. flags. Then we would sing our theme song, "Onward Christian Soldiers". Then we had a short lesson about a piece of our armor from Ephesians 6:11-18 in the New Testament Bible. After that, we would go to class with kids from our age group and do crafts. Wednesday evening was another repeat of Sunday morning and evening church services "sleep or read", but be quiet. Do not let me forget that Tuesday afternoon, an elderly missionary lady would come to our house and teach Bible lessons to a few kids from the neighborhood, my sisters, brother and me. That would consume most of that afternoon.

I had one sister two years older than me, one sister two years younger, and a brother four years younger. After church on Sunday morning, Mom made sure that her children kept the Sabbath day holy. The word "no" best describes how she made sure that we did that. No swimming, no fishing, no anything that was fun! If you wanted a spanking, sass her, say darn, damn, Hell, or Jeez. Mom's kids were going to go to Heaven even if she had to scare the Hell out of us to get us there. On weekdays before we could go to school, mom would have us kids form a circle in our living room and have family prayer. One by One we would ask God to watch over us as we went through our day. And as if praying before going to school was not enough, my mom had us pray a blessing over all of our meals, and we prayed together before going to bed. The prayers I wanted to keep private I prayed quietly in my bedroom. I prayed when I did something wrong, I prayed for people that I thought were doing something wrong, and I prayed for help to keep us from doing something wrong.

In the summer when we had vacation from school, mom would have us go to Vacation Bible School. We liked that because there were a lot of crafts, and we could win prizes if we learned the books of the bible and bible verses. A car would drive through our neighborhood with a loudspeaker yelling the day and hour the bible school bus would start picking us up. That school lasted one week. Then mom would take us to Grandma's house to go to Vacation Bible School at her church. Grandma had twelve kids which meant that I had a lot of cousins that would go to her house for Vacation Bible School with us. We would all sleep in tents and for one more week we would learn bible verses, books of the bible, and win more prizes.

When I turned eight, I was old enough to go to C.Y.C. camp. This was another time of Bible lessons and crafts, but this time we got to go swimming. We also stayed in cabins at the campground for three days and nights. Most of the time we did all of the activities by age groups which ranged from eight to fourteen. There were meetings in the evenings where everyone in camp attended one large service together. As If all of these church functions were not enough, we also had to go to revivals once a year. We would have a week of revival at our church, then a week of revival at grandma's church.

The Bible says in **Proverbs 22:6** "Train **up a child** in the way he should go, **and** even when he is old he will not depart from it". My mother was doing her best to train us up to be good Christian children, but she could not be with us every minute of every day. The Bible also says in **2 Corinthians 6:14** "Be not **unequally yoked** with unbelievers: for what fellowship have righteousness and iniquity? Or what communion hath light with darkness?" Everything my mother, my pastor, and my Christian teachers were trying to teach me was not affecting my behavior as much as what I was learning from my cousins, friends, and classmates.

Let me start with cousins. I was five years old when my aunt caught me underneath the bed with her daughter. We were looking at each other's private parts. My aunt knew that I was terrified of her false teeth. I was okay as long as they were in her mouth, but when she took them out I panicked. My aunt pulled me out from underneath the bed with one arm, and pulled out her teeth with the other. She chased me down the stairs, through the living room, out the front door, and around the yard. I will never forget the image of my aunt chasing me with her piranha teeth, nor will I ever forget the image that I saw underneath the bed. This would be my first Spiritual battle that I can remember and the root of every battle thereafter.

My friends should have been put in a room alone with my mother where she could have interrogated them. All of them would have confessed and pled guilty to escape the questioning. All my mother would have had to do is come out to our fort and I would have been put in solitary confinement for the rest of my life. Even though we stole all of the building materials from old project houses and other available places, my mother would not have questioned that. Wall to wall carpeting and furniture also would most likely have escaped questioning. The only thing that my mother would have seen was our wallpaper. About 400 square ft. of naked woman embraced our forts' décor. As you can see from this, I lost my first Spiritual battle.

My classmates: I was in the fifth grade when I got my first reality check on how not to be popular. My class was having a talent show and all of us had to participate. My teacher saw that the new kid, Ed, and I were lost on what we would do. She being the up-to-date person who knew all of the trendy stuff that kids were doing decided to put Ed and me together as a duet. She even picked the song that we would sing: "He's got the Whole World in His Hands". While practicing, I thought that Ed and I were going to be great. We knew all of the words and we sounded good.

The big day came for the big show. I was nervous and excited at the same time. My classmates brought in records by the Beatles, the Rolling Stones, and Herman's Hermits to play as they sang along with them. This was great and the classroom was rocking. Nothing could ruin this day. It was time for Ed and me to keep the excitement going. We sang out, He's got the Whole World in His Hands". The room was silent, and then it was filled with laughter. Our classmates were not laughing for us. They were laughing at us! They all thought that we were a joke. After school that day, I ran home so I would not be seen by anyone. This was my second most embarrassing thing that ever happened at school. My first was in the third grade when my music teacher blew on her kazoo and said this is the note we start on, and I farted thunder at the same moment.

I wanted to quit school and join the foreign legion, but I was only ten. This really wrecked my game [as if a ten year old has game]! Up to now, all of my performing was done at church or at home where I never was humiliated no matter how bad I sounded. Was this response from my classmates because of something I did or because of someone I believed in? Now I was facing another huge battle. Do I want to be popular at school "which would be impossible now", or bring what I was taught at church to school?

My mother would have had to lock her children in their bedrooms to train us up in the way the Bible says, even the living room would have had to be off limits. The television shows were not as vulgar then as they are today, but they did promote some non-Christian programs. Bewitched and Disney both promoted witchcraft. Even the comic books we would read were contrary to our Christian belief in one God. Thor was the god of thunder; Superman had super powers, and even the cuddly little devil in diapers "hot stuff" turned Satan into a character that should be loved, like Casper the friendly ghost.

The Bible says in Mark 3:24 , "If a kingdom be divided against itself, that kingdom cannot stand". This verse is referring to the devil and his kingdom, but every person is a kingdom themselves. How are we supposed to stand, when everything we are taught to believe by our Christian teachers is being attacked by our family, friends, classmates, and the whole secular world?

CHAPTER TWO

TEENAGE TEMPTATIONS

The Bible says in **Matthew 26:41** "Watch and pray, that ye enter not into temptation: the spirit indeed is willing, but the flesh is weak". I must confess, in my early teens my spirit was not willing, and my flesh was weaker than weak. Whatever my flesh lusted for, I did. My secular training always won the battle. My Christian training would shift into gear after the fact, and I would repent {pray for forgiveness} when I felt guilty.

I was never allowed to drink alcohol growing up, not even a taste. I had my first drink when I stayed overnight at my friend Jacks house on New Year's Eve, when I was thirteen. We were able to drink some homemade wine that his dad made. I got a small buzz that night, and even had the opportunity to make out with his younger sister for a little while. The wine was ok, but kissing the girl was the best. That night was my first battle with alcohol. "I lost". I had a small hangover the next morning, but I could handle that. The only thing that I could not handle was the overwhelming desire to make out with my friend's sister again.

Jack was popular at school. Since I was his friend whenever kids from our school would throw a party, Jack would talk them into inviting me. The only refreshments at these parties were non-alcoholic. Kids would play spin the bottle for kisses which was ok, but when I played the game at home with friends and cousins, clothes came off. Most of the time when I went to one of these parties I would talk to the guys I knew. I wanted to talk to the girls, but just could not work up the courage.

I was still thirteen when Jack invited me to a party that he was going to go to at his neighbor's house. He said that there would be a lot of beer, and that after the party we could go camp out at our fort. He did not have to ask me twice. Two teenage girls lived at that house, and I figured that some of their friends would be there also. I could hardly wait for the weekend. I wasn't as excited about the booze as I was about the possibility that there might be some girls partying with us.

When I arrived at the party, I saw Jack and three of my other friends standing around a large washtub that was full of beer and ice. There were no girls with them. Jack failed to tell me that there was going to be a party inside the house with mostly adults and a couple of older teens. The five of us would have to party outside. I didn't like the taste of beer, but I drank it anyway. We drank a lot of beer before deciding that we would go out to our fort while we could still walk.

The fort was about a half mile walk from where we were. We stuffed our pockets with the leftover cold beers before leaving. The first part of our walk to the fort was on a dirt road that was easy to navigate because there was a street light on the corner. We were drunk, but we could still see where we were going. After walking the road for about two blocks, we turned onto a path that went through the woods to the railroad tracks. The light from the streetlight disappeared so we had to use our lighters and matches to find our way.

Once we made it to the tracks, our hike was about complete. We only had a block left to walk before we would be home safe. Our lighters were too hot to use for lighting and we were out of matches. We would have to walk the rest of the way in the dark. The beers kept falling out of our pockets, so we decide to lighten our load and bury the cans beside the path. We would mark the spots where we buried our treasure with an X so that we could find our stash in the morning. We were like life size marbles in a giant pin ball machine. The trees, bushes, and stumps were the bumpers. Whenever you hit a tree or bush, or fell over a stump you knew that you were off the path. The beer we drank even gave the game sound effects. It took a lot of bumper action, but we all finally made it to the fort.

There was a bunk bed and a couch at the fort for three of us to sleep on. The other two would have to get as comfortable as they could on the floor. Jack grabbed the couch; Jim claimed the bottom bunk and I climbed onto the top bunk. If my other two friends felt as bad as I did, they were thrilled just to be at the fort, and the floor would be a great place to die.

The night passed quickly. When I awoke, my head felt like there was someone trapped behind my forehead hammering against my skull for a way to escape. As if my head was not already taking a beating from the inside out, the outside going in was inflicting even more damage through my nose. Overnight, the fort had turned into an outhouse! All of my senses were coming alive at the same time. The cussing and gaging sounds coming from below were probably what woke me up in the first place.

My two friends who slept on the floor were covered with puke. There was so much of the smelly slime covering them that they looked like a couple of swamp creatures! All that I could think of, was how I was going to get out of the fort without any of the putrid vomit touching me. I cannot imagine what my two drenched friends felt like. After all, some of their new liquid attire was donated to them from above.

After we all made a flash exit from the fort, reality hit us. As sick as we all were, there was no going back into the fort to lie down. I would have to, hopefully, sneak into my house without being seen. Jack and Jim's parents probably would not care. And my other two friends would be lucky if their parents let them inside the house at all. We stopped on our way home to recover our buried treasures, but we could not find one X.

I swore then that I would never drink again. It was kind of like having the flu with a migraine headache. I lay in bed trying my best to fall asleep, but that wasn't happening.

Also, having to hide in my room made me have a heavy feeling of guilt. This time I knew that I had fought a battle and lost. Alcohol was a giant, and I was not a giant killer. The Bible warned me in **1 Peter 5:8** "Be sober, be watchful: your adversary the devil, as a **roaring lion**, walks about, seeking whom he may devour". It was too bad for me that I didn't take the time to read that. I would not have obeyed it, even if I did.

It was about this same time that my mom and dad divorced, and I will confess that my mother had her hands full with my sisters and brother without having to worry about me. She would send me to stay with relatives as much as possible. My family had quit going to church regularly. When I was fifteen, I would hitchhike ten miles to my cousin's house and spend a week or two at a time with them. There was a park nearby where we could swim and be with girls. On Friday nights, we could go to the dance and be with more girls.

I did not keep my oath to myself to never drink again. Usually when I drank, something bad happened, but nothing bad enough to make me quit. Fighting, getting drunk and kissing ugly girls was quickly becoming my weekend job. I was told a story about a guy who got so drunk that he went home with a really ugly girl. When he woke up the next morning the pitiful looking thing had her head resting on his arm. Rather than wake her up and have to talk to her, he bit off his arm and ran out of there. That should have been funny, but it just made me wonder how many one armed woman there were that woke up next to me?

I spent so much time away from home that when I ran away nobody missed me. My friends kept talking about the hippies in Haight Ashbury, California. If we got there, we could have all of the drugs, sex, and rock and roll that we wanted. My friend Dale and I decided that we would hitchhike there. We lived in Michigan, and we had no money but we didn't care. We started out on a country road in front of Dale's parents' house. We had to wait quite a while for a car to come by. We put our thumbs out, and the first car that came by stopped. There were three men in the car and they had an open case of beer. They were from Indianapolis Indiana and they offered us a beer and jobs carpeting hotels. We were off and running.

About a week later, I wrote to my mother and told her where I was and what I was doing. She didn't even know I was gone until she got the letter. A couple of weeks later we got fired. The boss said that the carpets were too short, but I knew it was because some money came up missing. I know, because I took it. Dale and I were back on the road again. We made it to Missouri before we stopped again. This time it was not willingly. The police guessed that I was a runaway and took me to jail. Dale was seventeen, so the police let him go. It took them five days to find out who I was and let me go. My mom sent money for my bus fare home, and the police made sure that I got on the bus.

When I got back home, my house was empty. My mother and new stepfather had moved. My mother found me later that day at Jack's house. We were now living in a house with no neighborhood. Twenty miles from the friends that I grew up with, and almost a mile from any house at all. I don't know for sure where I wanted to be at this point in my life, but I knew for sure that it was not there.

After a couple of months, a runaway boy moved in with his aunt at the house closest to ours. His aunt and my mother thought that I could be a friend for him and vice versa. They were right. We became good friends, but not exactly what my mother and his aunt had hoped for. Dan and I got along great because we both had the same attitude towards life. Nobody was going to tell us what to do!

A carnival came to a town nearby and I talked Dan into going with me to see if we could make some money setting up rides. The carnival was always looking for young guys to do the heavy work assembling the rides. I had done this before but this time they wanted us to stay after setting up. We were asked to keep working for the two weeks that the carnival was going to be in town. That sounded good to us. I loved the work and the fringe benefits. There were girls hustling us for free rides, and we would hustle them for everything else.

When it came time for the carnival to leave and go to another town, they said I could travel with them if I got a note from my parents. It would be a few months before I would be sixteen so I needed their permission. My mother knew that it would do her no good to try and stop me, so she consented to let me go.

I came back home after a couple of months of traveling. The carnival was a lot more work and a lot more trouble than I expected. I had to sleep under rides and in trucks. The pay was terrible, so I would steal from the stores in towns where we went. There was always someone to steal from me. The only thing I was going to miss was the girls that were always available.

Being back home was relaxing at first, but after a week it just got boring. Summer was over and Dan was in school. I decided that I would go back to school just for something to do. This would be a new school and my second year in the ninth grade. I was almost sixteen in a freshman class. I skipped classes, smoked cigarettes, and I still had that "nobody is telling me what to do attitude".

I was in the principal's office regularly, and teachers usually just put up with me. Even my classmates left me alone. There was a small group of us that were "authority challenged", and we would push people in authority to their limits.

Once in a while, we could even make other students dislike us because of our behavior. Butch was one of those boys who hated me because I was not like him. Butch excelled in sports, he got good grades, he was muscular, good looking, popular, and his parents had money. He had everything that I didn't have. My friends warned me that Butch was telling everyone that he was going to kick my butt. When I would see Butch walking down the hallways in school, he would try his best to pretend that he did not see me. I guess it was just talk.

I had made a few friends when I went to school, but that winter I quit anyway. Whenever I got the chance, I would go hang out with them. Ryan was one of those new friends who influenced me the most. Up to now, I did all of my partying with alcohol. Ryan loved his beer, but he liked his weed just as much. It was just a matter of time before I started smoking weed too. It seemed like every time we smoked pot, there were girls wanting to get high with us. My mother had warned me about drugs, but I was more afraid of being alone. I had drugs, sex, and rock & roll now, and I didn't have to run away to find them.

When school let out for the summer, a bunch of us decided to go camping at a county park at Lake Michigan. That ended up being the most fun that I had ever had. We camped there most of the summer. The first week or two we all camped in one huge tent. When other friends found out that we were partying hard at our campsite, they came out to camp with us. In a few short weeks, we went from five or six campers in one tent to thirty campers in a bunch of tents. This was more than just camping. It was the biggest and longest party I had ever seen. On weekend's friends of all of these friends joined in. Along with all the new people, came new and harder drugs.

There was one church service that I could not shake as I was making my decision whether or not to take the harder drugs. Four teens came to our church one Sunday to give us their testimonies. One of them said the words that I never forgot . He said that his addiction cost him two hundred dollars a day. How could a person spend that much money on drugs? I did not know it, but the decision I made now would affect everything I did for the rest of my life. One weekend someone brought out enough mescalines so that anyone who wanted to buy some could. Two dollars a hit didn't seem like too much money for something that was going to keep you stoned for hours. I lost another battle! I took a pill and loved it. I don't know why I was so worried.

We started a huge game of Frisbee before the drugs started to affect us. The rules were, if you tried to catch the Frisbee and missed you were out. When the mescaline started working, it was great. I had never seen such beautiful colors come alive. The Frisbees were glowing with trails behind them. The sky, the grass and even the people had a florescent-like glow to them. We were laughing so hard that we had all we could do to keep from getting sick. I loved it. I had never been this high before, and there was no hangover.

Ryan and I got jobs trimming Christmas trees. This was hard work in direct sunlight. We had razor sharp knives that we would use to shape the fir trees. We had to walk around each tree and swing the knives along the outside taking off just the longest buds. That would stop the growth of that branch and the shorter ones would grow out to fill in the bare spots to form a beautiful Christmas tree. There could be a few hundred trees in each row, and we would trim a row in a couple of hours. By the end of an eight hour day, we were hot and exhausted. One evening after a blistering day of work, Ryan suggested that we buy some beer. We had enough money for two cases.

We were too young to buy alcohol, but there were a couple of old retired dudes that lived in Ryan's dad's garage that would probably purchase the beer for us. Oscar and Dick were alcoholics, and most likely broke. They were both already drunk and out of money. We were an answer to their prayers. Oscar said that he would buy if Ryan or I rode with him. Dick told Ryan that Oscar was too drunk to drive, and that he was not to go. Dick didn't know me so he didn't care if I went.

Oscar was a big man and as rough as they came. He had an indent in his forehead where he had been shot. You could see his heartbeat behind the layer of skin that covered the cavity. I rode with Oscar once before when he was drinking, and he drove a little bit fast, but he stayed on the road. I agreed to ride along and off we went. Oscar had a 1960 big black Oldsmobile. The closest place to buy beer was at the Shamrock Inn about three miles away. Oscar tore out of the driveway and onto the pavement. About a block away was a semi-truck and flatbed trailer parked on the side of the road. Oscar didn't even see it. I yelled and Oscar swerved just enough to keep us from smashing into the back of the trailer's bed.

There was a stop sign about a hundred yards in front of the truck, and Oscar stopped for it just like he knew what he was doing. I thought about getting out of the car but once Oscar made his turn it would be a straight shot to the bar. Oscar hit the straight away and the gas pedal at the same time. He kept the pedal down until we reached about eighty miles an hour. There was a car coming toward us in the opposite lane. Oscar decided that he would share the lane with the oncoming car. I screamed as loud as I could and Oscar swerved in the nick of time again. I can't speak for the people in the other car, but I think that they thought that they were dead too. I don't know how we kept from hitting them head on. Then he turned in front of another oncoming car to get in his own lane.

The rest of the ride was pavement and gravel, but at least he stayed on his side of the road. Oscar turned into the bar parking lot and stopped the car. He went in to buy the beer, and I sat in the car with what should have been an easy decision to make. I should have jumped out of the car and got out of there as fast as I could, but I convinced myself that Oscar would have killed himself if I was not there. What could I do? I saved his life and besides that if I walked back most of the beer would be gone. When Oscar returned, I was stupidly still sitting there waiting for him. I asked if I could drive back, but found out that Oscar really got mad when you suggested that he could not drive. I should not have asked to drive. Oscar sped out of the parking lot angry and drunk. Where was a cop when you needed one? We were about a mile from the bar and the speedometer read ninety mph. That was the last thing that I remember. I thought that I heard screeching tires, but I can't be too sure about that.

The next thing I remember was Ryan's dad screaming at me. He was blaming me for his friend's death. He said that Oscar got his head chopped off. I didn't have a clue what he was talking about. Then I panicked! I wasn't dreaming, and I wasn't in my bed. I was lying in a bathtub that was red with blood and there were people staring at me. An ambulance had just gotten there, and the paramedics were going to rush me to the hospital. I can't remember the ride to the hospital. Next thing I knew the doctor was telling me that this was going to hurt. I had a concussion, and he was going to have to put some stitches in my head without any  local anesthetic. The nurse volunteered to hold my hand while the doctor did his sewing. Fortunately, for the nurse, Ryan entered the room just as she was falling to her knees from the pain of me squeezing her hand. Ryan gave me his hand to let me hold and gave the nurse a break. As the doctor finished up his stitching, Ryan went down to his knees also.

My mother and sister were in my room when I woke up the next day. Mom said that she was taking my dad to work when she passed the wreck. She told my dad that she knew that I was in the accident, and that if I was she would come and get him at work. Mom and my sister didn't stay long. As they were leaving, I asked to see a mirror. Mom said that she would bring one tomorrow. The hospital released me the next day. Mom let me look into her mirror just as she promised. My nose was broken, I had two black eyes and I had stitches in my forehead. I actually looked better than I thought I would.

On the way home, we had to pass the salvage yard where the wrecker towed Oscar's car. Mom asked me if I wanted to see the car. I should have said no. I broke down in tears when I looked at it. The wrecker had to haul it in two pieces. All four tires were ripped off the car on impact, and the motor went through the car and into the trunk. I found out that the bathtub that I woke up in was at a friend's house. The tree was in his front yard. He told the police that he seen me crawl out of the wreckage. The police thought that I would have had to have been thrown from the car to live through the accident.

When I think about the accident, I thank God for hearing my mother's prayers of protection over me. Hitting a tree at ninety miles an hour and ripping the car apart was enough to kill anybody. To stay in the car while the engine and all of its wiring passed me was even more amazing. I was not near as grateful as I should have been. Within a couple of weeks, I looked like my old self again. I was still pretty even with a broken nose!

SPIRITUAL WARFARE THE BATTLE

When I got out of the hospital, I swore that I would never drink again. But I would not have been in the car with Oscar if I would have kept my promise to myself to quit drinking when I had such a bad hangover at my fort when I was younger. What would it take for me to turn my life around? After entering into the enemy's camp and being enticed by his overwhelming temptations, is it even possible for me to escape the devil's grip? The Bible says in **Ephesians 6:12** "For our wrestling is not against flesh and blood, but against the **principalities**, against the powers, against the world-rulers of this darkness, against the spiritual hosts of wickedness in the heavenly places". I was going to need help!

My sobriety lasted only a few weeks. If I had to choose one verse from the Bible that could have helped me if I obeyed it, it would be **2 Corinthians 6:14** "Be not **unequally yoked** with unbelievers: for what fellowship have righteousness and iniquity? Or what communion hath light with darkness?"

In the movie Forrest Gump; Forest says his mommy told him that stupid is what stupid does. That's not even scripture, but it sure described me.

I was living back home with my mom and stepdad. It was snowing and my whole day consisted of cutting, hauling, and stacking firewood. I worked hard, but when I asked my stepdad for five dollars so that I could go to a dance that Friday night he said no. That afternoon I got a phone call from Dan. He asked me if I wanted to make some money. I told him yes, and he and a guy I had never met before came to my house and picked me up. The friend's name was Clyde and he drove an older truck. Dan told me that there was a safe in a school about fifteen miles from us that they were going to go try to crack, and that it would take three of us to do it.

Why not? I had no money for the dance, and here was my chance to get some. The fast money at the school was a joke. The safe was huge and inexperienced burglars were not going to get into it. We settled for change from the vending machines and a couple of cases of pop. All of that work, and I was still not going to the dance. On the way back we passed a grocery store that was just begging to become our next target. The lighting was poor so we pulled the truck right up to the back door. We were in luck. All that was stopping us from going in was a piece of plywood blocking the entrance. This was going to be quick and easy. The bed of the truck was about two feet from the now open store doorway. The whisky and wine shelves were only ten feet from the truck. Beer was next to them, and there were cigarettes just on the other side of the aisle. We loaded the back of the truck with cases of alcohol, cartons of cigarettes, huge bags of candy bars and were back on the road in minutes. By this time, we were so buzzed up from the robberies that a gas station just outside our hometown could not be passed up. We got more cigarettes and cash that was stashed in a vending machine.

We thought that we were super thieves now. We decided to break into another gas station right in town. There were display shelves inside with cigars, lighters, and an assortment of other items.
We filled boxes with the stuff not even caring what was going into them. We left there, and decided that we had enough. Clyde said he knew a girl close by who would stash our stolen treasures for us if we were willing to share some of the goods with her. Clyde was right. Except for a few bottles of wine, we carried the rest of the boxes into his friend's house. We stayed at her house for a little while when we were finished unloading. We had to sample some of the wine. Dan got drunk, and he wanted a ride home. That was the last thing that I wanted to do. Dan's whining finally got to us, and we took him home.

I called my mom from Dan's aunt's house and told her that a friend was going to loan me some money to buy some coal so I would not have to cut wood today. I told her that I would get it when the hardware opened at nine o'clock .It was about seven now. Mom knew that something wasn't right.

Clyde and I had a good buzz going by now and we decided to return to his friend's house and party with her for a couple of hours until we could buy some coal. I thought that Clyde was an idiot, but he proved to be dumber than I thought. He spun a donut with his truck in front of a police car. When the officer saw the stuff in the back of the truck and the condition that we were in, he arrested us. We went straight to jail.

This was it! I finally had enough. I had my mom's pastor come visit me, and I asked God to forgive me. I promised that I would not drink again. I started reading my Bible and praying to be free every day. Finally after forty five days in jail, I was going to get to see the judge. The guard took me down to a holding cell were I could change into my street clothes before seeing the magistrate. Clyde was there too. This was the first time that I saw him since we were arrested, and he was stealing my boots. Now, I knew that my first impression of him was true. He was an idiot.

Clyde and I went into the courtroom together. The judge had us stand in front of his bench as he scolded us. He said that he could understand us stealing the alcohol; he could even understand us stealing the money, but two thousand contraceptives. We must have planned a wild sex life. The court room roared with laughter. I turned my head to see that my mom was laughing too. That just wasn't right. The judge sentenced us to four years of probation.

My probation officer gave me my rules. I had to be in my house by midnight. I had to report to him every month. I had to pay five hundred dollars restitution over the next four years, and I had to go back to school. Then he showed me a big photograph of Jackson prison. He told me that he could put me there if I violated any of the conditions of my probation. I assured him that was not going to happen.

I started attending church that Sunday with full intention of starting a new life. It did not take me long to find out that this would be impossible if I was not willing to give up my old one. Dan and I would go to his cousin's house on weekends. Everyone there drank alcohol, and they always offered me some. I refused for a couple of months, but after a while the temptation ended up being too much for me, and the memories of jail faded away.

One Friday night Dan and I got Jeff, a friend of ours, to drive us to Dan's cousin's house. Jeff had an antique 1940s Buick. It was black and big enough to party in. We picked up some quarts of beer and two girls that were friends with Dan's cousins joined us. Dan and Jeff sat in the front seat with one girl and I sat in back with the other. It was winter so John kept the car running. The next thing I knew, I woke up in the hospital. Dan said that he thought that Mandy and I were clowning around in the back seat, when we were actually being poisoned by carbon-monoxide. This was my first time drinking since going to jail, and I was already in a hospital.

It wasn't long, and I started treating my probation like a joke. Being seventeen and having to sit in a classroom with a bunch of freshman was my first defiance of my probation officer's rules. I was told to spit out my gum in a science class, and I refused. The teacher said to spit it out or for me to get out. I went out. The principal said that he had enough of my rebellion, and kicked me out of school. When my probation officer asked me about school on my next visit to his office, he scolded me and again showed me the photograph of Jackson prison.

By that next summer, I was back to drinking whenever I had the opportunity. I lived with Dan's cousin's part time and I totally ignored my probation's curfews. I was a lot smarter than the law, and I would prove it. There was going to be a huge party a couple of blocks from where I was staying with Dan's cousins, and there was an alley that went from their house to the house where the party was. I could not have planned this any better myself. I went to the party knowing that I could drink as much as I wanted, then just walk the alley back home.

The plan was great, but the execution of the plan had its flaws. The alley was dark and I was smashed. As I was stumbling home, I hit something solid and fell on top of it. When I looked up I thought, no way possible. You have got to be kidding me! There were two police officers on the other side of the windshield laughing hysterically. I couldn't run. I could not even get off the hood of their car without their help. I cried as I explained my situation in an attempt to escape arrest, but they were not falling for my lame excuses. On my way to jail, they informed me that they were just taking a break. They could have picked a different location!

I spent three days in jail, and I had to pay a fine for public intoxication. I'm glad that it was not a crime for being stupid. I would still be there. My probation officer scolded me again and said that he would be merciful and let me off with time served, and, of course, another look at the photograph of Jackson prison. I don't think that I even tried to quit drinking this time.

About six months later, Ryan invited me to a party that was going to be held in a small town about twenty miles away. He told me that there would be a lot of girls there. Ryan's older brother, Jake, was going to drive and he was also going to buy a couple of cases of beer. Jeff's girlfriend and her younger sister would also ride with us. Both of them were juveniles. Our friend Dale decided to park his car and ride with us. Altogether, there would be six of us going. We stopped at a bar on the way and Jeff picked up two cases of beer and put them in the trunk. Once we were out of town, Jeff pulled to the side of the road and got six beers out of the trunk. There was one for each of us. We went a few miles further up the road and the thing that I feared the most happened.

Why was it that every time I was doing something illegal, these idiots were there to stop me? Lights flashing, sirens screaming, spotlight shining, and me drinking. What was a boy to do? I looked for a place to hide my bottle, and then I just prayed that the officers miscounted. I told them that I was not drinking, but six people with six opened bottles exposed my lie. Jeff got a ticket for contributing to the delinquency of minors, Dale and I got tickets for minors in possession, and Ryan and the two sisters were juveniles so the cops gave them a chewing out. The police ordered us to pour out all of the beers on the ground. Even the unopened ones were uncapped and emptied.

We had to wait two weeks for our court date, so that gave me plenty of time to report this to my probation officer. Yea, like that was going to happen! I decided to take my chances and hope that he did not find out. For the next two weeks, I prayed. Lord let me get away with this, and I will never drink again. The judge sentence Jake to fifteen days in jail, and Dale and I had to be locked up for seven. The three of us shared the same cell. The judge never mentioned a thing about my probation, so I thought that there was a possibility that he did not know. I was in a jail in a different county and I might have gotten away with the cover up.

On the seventh day a guard came and got Dale and me so that we could both be released. So I thought; I was half right. Dale went home, but there was a police officer from the county that I lived in standing at the counter. He told me that he was there to give me a ride to see my probation officer. I asked the officer what he thought was going to happen to me? He said that most likely my P.O. just wants to talk to me. He was right. After I spent forty five more days in jail, my P.O. finally talked to me. He said that he hoped that I had learned something, and that if I got caught drinking again he would make sure that I went to prison. And yes, he showed me a picture of Jackson prison again.

I would have been caught again, but the drinking age was lowered from twenty-one to eighteen. I was still on probation when I got my first driving permit. I would not have gotten my driver's license or kept my freedom if it was not for the leniency of the police officer at my next violation giving me a second chance. This officer pulled me over for driving while intoxicated the minute I left the bar. He asked me for my driver's license, and I handed him a dollar bill. He told me that it was an awful small bribe. To make me look stupider than I already did, I tried to explain that I just had my permit and it was on paper also. The officer asked me where I was headed and I pointed at a house about a hundred yards away. He said that he was going to give me a break. He let a passenger in my car drive to the house I pointed at and park it. He warned me that if he saw that car again that night that he would arrest me. I was lucky this time. The police let me go and my P.O. never found out about it.

My teenage years were years of rebellion. I rebelled against every kind of authority there was. I rebelled against the legal system, against the school system, and against my Christian upbringing.

The Bible said this about rebellion when Samuel confronted king Saul: **Samuel 15:23** "For rebellion is as the sin of witchcraft, and stubbornness is as idolatry

CHAPTER THREE

ROARING TWENTIES THE EARLY YEARS

Hard to believe that I survived my teen years, but that was nothing compared to my next ten years. Let me tell you about them! I got a job at a local saw mill and an apartment above the local bar in town. Whenever I had the money, I was drinking alcohol, smoking weed, or both. Any thoughts of going straight and returning to a life of morality had long past. My years on probation were complete and I had stayed out of jail for a few years. The only time I called on God was when I was in trouble, and right now the devil was lying to me telling me everything was alright.

My friend, Lee, would come get me on weekends so that we could party and booze cruise. Lee liked to drink tequila straight and eat mescaline. We would ride around the country roads getting high. If we needed to rest, we would go back to my house.

Lee flew to Texas on weekdays, and he would pick up a car and drive it back to Michigan. He never questioned what was being transported in the vehicles. He got paid three thousand dollars every time he made this trip. That was all that he cared about. Sometimes he did these trips twice in one week. I made about one hundred dollars a week busting my butt at the saw mill, and Lee was making thousands sitting on his. He tried his best to talk me into quitting my job and come work with him. It was tempting, but I knew what would happen if I got caught.

I was shooting pool at a local tavern one night, and Lee came in obviously drunk already. He told me that he needed my help to pull his car out of a ditch. We drove a quarter of a mile from the bar and Lee said to stop by the creek. He said the car is down there. No way! There was no way that we were going to get the car out of there without a wrecker. Lee agreed and said lets go back to the bar, I will buy another one tomorrow. The car he was driving was a black MG convertible. Now, I was thinking, maybe I should work for his boss. It was just a couple of weeks later that Lee came to my house in a panic. I had never seen him like this. He said that I was right when I told him I wouldn't quit my job. He told me that he tried to quit, but his employer told him if he did, he would kill him or somebody in his family. He said that his employer showed him pictures of his mother, father, brothers and sister. Lee was not a person who scared easily, but this time you could see the fear in him.

I had not seen Lee in a long time. When I ran into his brother, I found out why. Lee quit driving for his employer and went to another state to hide out. Lee's employer found out where he was hiding, and killed him. I guess it was better for Lee to die than his whole family.

I tried not to have parties at my house, but one night it could not be avoided. Late one evening there was a knock at my door and a whole bunch of my friends who I had not seen in years were looking for a place to party. I don't even know how they found out where I lived. They were making way too much noise in the hallway so I let them come in, and I tried to quiet them down.

It was odd enough to see this group of old friends, but it was even weirder to see who they had brought with them. It was Butch. Remember the jock from school who wanted to fight me? Here he was, in my house, and he was partying with my friends. I was dumbfounded. Actually, Butch was the only one of the bunch that behaved. He just sat there quietly and drank his beer. He even toked on the weed when it was passed his way. The party was short. When the beer was gone, everyone left. That whole night freaked me out.

A couple of weeks later there was a knock on my door, and this time I was really caught off guard. There in my hallway stood Butch with a pretty young girl whom I assumed was his girlfriend. Butch asked me if he could come in and smoke some weed. I let them come in, and we smoked a few joints. Butch talked and acted like we had been friends for years while his girlfriend just sat there quietly. After a couple of hours, they left. If I had learned anything about hanging around people who got stoned, anything can happen.

I got a phone call from Dan a couple of days after partying with Butch and his girlfriend. Dan told me that Butch got stoned on acid, and that he could not handle it. He took a broken bottle and brutally murdered his girlfriend. I pray that it did not happen the same night that they came to my house. I did not try to find out, and I never want to. I already lived with enough guilt; I did not need any more.

Let me think about this for a minute. Oscar lost his head, I was in jail three times, Lee got murdered, and Butch murdered his girlfriend. I had to be the loneliest person on earth. Every girl I ever dated left me, my marriage ended in divorce, and I was a deadbeat dad. NOW, would be a good time to turn from my destructive lifestyle. NOW, would be the perfect time to pray. YOU THINK?

I was twenty one years old and I was a mess. I decided to ask my friends Joe and Jim if I could stay and work with them. They were roofers and they always needed someone to labor for them. Jobs were scarce, so we had more days' off-the-job than we had on. If we did hustle up a job, it usually kept us busy for a couple of days. We would get paid and go straight to the bar, and spend all of our earnings the same day that we got it. Then for the next week or two, we would try to find more work.

There was a small county park with a nice beach just a few miles from where we stayed. Joe and I would spend a lot of our time relaxing there on our jobless days. Joe was a couple of years younger than me, but he was a seasoned alcoholic. I could handle sitting at the park and watching the young girls in their tiny bikinis, but I could not handle being broke.

Joe had another brother named Jesse. Jessie was in college but he stayed in the same room with Joe and me at their mom's house. Jessie asked me if I wanted to sell some weed for him so that I could have some money. I told him that I would take a couple of dime bags to the park with me and see what I could do. A dime bag sold for ten dollars. There were a lot of people that hung around the park, but I didn't know any of them. If I was going to sell some weed, I was going to need some help.

I would have to find a person who looked like he was a drug user. There was a girl that hung out at the park every day. She looked like what I envisioned a hippie to look like. She had straggly red hair, cutoff jeans, and mirrored sunglasses. There was usually a bunch of teenagers hanging around with her. I went up to her and asked her if she wanted to smoke a joint? We fired one up, and I almost did what I set out to do. But instead of selling weed to make my friend Jesse and me money, I smoked the weed, and it ended up costing Jesse money.

I fit right in with Red and her group of friends. So, I made myself a permanent resident. The park was open from 10:00 AM to 10:00 PM 7 days a week in the summer. What should have been prime working hours was prime partying time for most of us. Red had a car and when the park got crowded with families trying to enjoy the picnic area and the beach, we would go for short rides away from everyone so that we could smoke dope without causing trouble.

On one of those congested days, Red asked Fred to join us for a reefer ride .Fred lived with his mother who had a house about a city block from the park. He was the parks' handyman. If leaves needed raked, or lawns needed mowing, Fred was the man for the job. Fred looked like a cave man. He had long curly frizzy light brown hair with a beard to match. He was short and stocky and usually wore a pair of cut-off blue jeans and no shirt.

We decided to drive the back roads about five miles away from the park and smoke a joint as we cruised. When we turned around to go back to the park, the fuel pump took a dump. We had a hose to siphon gas from the gas tank, and a beer can to hold the gas, but we needed a way to get the gas from the can into the carburetor. It took a little bargaining, but Fred volunteered to be the fuel pump if we gave him a couple of joints when we got back to the park.

Fred hopped on the fender of the car and reached underneath the open hood to prepare himself for Red's signal to start pouring. Red waved Fred on as she turned the key in the ignition. It worked! Red must have done this before? Maybe not! About a mile from the park, the carburetor backfired and Fred flew off the fender and into the ditch. When Fred stood up, we knew that he was okay. We had to laugh! Fred's hair on his head and face was a little more frizzed now than it was when we left the park.

Red and I knew that getting Fred back underneath that hood was not going to be easy. But we were only one mile from the park, so we had to think of something. Forget the fact that Fred could have been seriously hurt, or killed, that was secondary. We told Fred that we would give him more weed if he tried again. That didn't work. How about more weed and a plastic bottle instead of a can? That worked! Fred jumped back onto the fender, and positioned himself underneath the hood for another try. Red gave the signal and we were off. This time we could see the park in the distance when the carburetor back fired. Fred flew off the fender and into the ditch again. This time when he stood up he looked like he had put his head in an open flame. He was a mess. Fortunately, we were close enough to the park to get help to push the car the rest of the way. Everything turned out fine. Fred got his weed, and we all made it back to the park.

Ralph came walking up to us, and he looked worse than Fred. Ralph was complaining that some dude named Sam sucker punched him at the bar. Ralph's eye looked terrible. It was shining with the brightest purples, blues and yellows, all mixed together. Ralph was a self-proclaimed tough guy. Ralph looked like he could fight but looks are deceiving. Ralph started bragging that when he saw Sam again that he was going to get even. As fate would have it, it was only minutes before Sam's van entered the park.

Sam parked by the entrance, so Ralph was going to have to back up his mouth and confront Sam there. It did not take long and Ralph was back. This time Ralph's eyes were a matching set. I had to admit, what Ralph lacked in his ability to fight he made up for with courage. I would have quit after the first black eye. I explained to Ralph the basics of fighting. You make your hand into a fist and punch your opponent in the eye. You do not take your eye and run it into your opponent's fist. I shut up after I saw that all I was doing was getting Ralph mad at me, and he was in no condition to defend his honor. Ralphs younger sister, Tonya, tries her best to act like her older brother. We all put up with her because she usually comes to buy a couple of joints then leaves. If only she could see her brother now.

That was the first time that I had ever seen Sam. From what I was hearing, I most likely did not want to meet him. Sam and his friends in the van had stolen a safe with five thousand dollars in it a couple of days earlier.

Sam took some of the money and bought the van, and the rest of the money was paying for the booze and drugs that they were partying with.

When the park closes, our daytime home closes with it. There are a lot of two-tracks and partying spots in the woods close by, and all we have to do is decide where to meet. On weekdays, there might be ten of us at one of these locations, but on weekends that number could be in the fifties. A few of us called these spots home.

One Friday, Ralph drove into the park in a new Toyota which his mother signed for. There was going to be a huge party at the turn-around at the end of Drakes Rd. that night, and Ralph asked me if I wanted to ride out there with him. We pulled in on the two track and both of us gasped. We had never seen this many people at one of these parties before. We were going to have to search for a place to park.

This was a two keg party with enough people to consume them quickly. We were not there but a few minutes, and people were already passing the hat to buy more beer. A car raced up the two-track and parked right next to the bonfire. I already knew that that had to be Steve. Steve had a garage at his mother's house where he and his friends did mechanic body work and painted cars. Steve made sure that his ride was fast and pretty. Steve and I were not close friends, but we shared one thing in common. Steve liked to do drugs and I liked to sell them.

I couldn't tell you how many kegs we went through that night. Matter of fact, most of the night was a blur. I woke up early the next morning in the front seat of Ralph's new car and Ralph was passed out behind his steering wheel. I don't remember how I got there or when. All of the other partiers had left. The only two people left in the woods were Ralph and me. My head was pounding and my pants were soaked because I pissed in them while I was passed out. The last thing I wanted to do was sit in the woods and wait for Ralph to wake up. I shook him and woke him up. He instantly started the car, put it in reverse and crashed into one of the trees behind us. That angered him enough to slam the car into drive and slam into a tree in front of us. Another quick shift into reverse and the tail-light on the opposite side of the car from the first smashed tail-light was demolished.

Ralph finally got his new car back onto the two-track, but not until his new Toyota looked like a beat up piece of scrap metal. Ralph dropped me off at the park, and that was the last time that I ever saw the Toyota. Ralph was a good friend so I saw him a lot after that, but the car and that morning was never brought up in conversation. It was as if it never happened.

The summer was there and gone in a flash. I managed to make it through without having to work a day, but now I knew that I would have to do something. My friend, Chip, suggested that we get jobs at the celery farm. I envied Chip. He had it all. He was about seventeen, and he had his own car and a great relationship with a beautiful girl. Chip drank a little beer and smoked a little grass but he did not let them control him. We worked there for a couple of weeks but, as soon as I got money for more drugs I quit.

After a few more weeks of being broke, Red suggested picking apples for some cash. Fred and Walt decided that they would tag along and pick apples with us. You already met Fred, the fuel pump. Even though Walt partied with us through the summer, there was nothing that I could really say about him. Walt was one of those guys that never said much. He would get high and sit back and listen while everyone else talked.

We all met at the orchard before daylight so we could smoke a joint before picking. About the second week on the job, Walt did not show up. We found out later that day that Walt's girlfriend broke up with him the night before. Walt was not one to drink much alcohol, but he wanted to get drunk and try not to think about his girlfriend leaving him. My friend who was with Walt said that later that night Walt said he was going in the house and going to bed. My friend asked Walt if he was sure that he was okay, and Walt said not to worry, that he was fine.

Walt went into his house, grabbed his gun and shot himself in the head. I could not believe that Walt did that. This was only the second time that I had heard about someone taking their own life. The first time was a kid in the fifth grade who hung himself because he had bad grades in school. Not one of these reasons made sense to me.

The last big party of the year was Halloween night. There were mummies, vampires, hookers, and people who did not dress up but looked as though they did. This was another night where any drug you wanted was most likely there. Brian was there with his wife who was an attractive girl. Problem was that Brian was jealous and tried to pick a fight with anyone who looked at her. When it was time for Brian to go before someone hurt him, Brian decided that he would drive his motorcycle home. Everyone at the party tried to talk him out of it. A lot of us offered to drive him home. There was no talking any sense into him. Brian tried to take a curve driving way too fast. The bike spilled and Brains' legs got tangled in its spokes. Brian had to have both of his legs amputated.

I got into a skilled trade school for the winter so Ryan and I decided to rent a house together. Since we had the house the only logical thing to do was to have a New Year's Eve party. I will just mention the highlights. Ralph got drunk and jealous of a girl that I dated but I really did not have strong feelings for at all. He decided that he would put on his superman costume just like he did with Sam when he fought with his face. Again, Ralph was not content with one black eye, so he asked me outside twice.

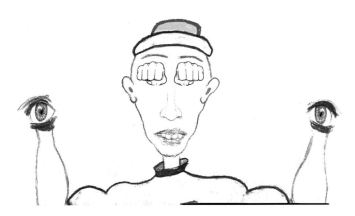

Someone decided to play spin the bottle for drinks in the living room. If the bottle landed on you, you had to chug down a beer. When the first person got sick and vomited on the floor, someone was actually sober enough to bring in a garbage can for the rest of the game. You would not believe how full the can got before the game ended. Happy New Year!

As soon as the snow was gone, I grabbed a tent and went camping at a secluded lake deep in the woods. When Red found out where I was camped she decided to come and join me. I smoked weed, and did a few hard drugs through the years but that was nothing compared to the partying that I was going to do this summer. We started out with a quiet campsite on a quiet lake, at a very relaxing scenic spot. It turned into a very noisy, hell raising party in just a few weeks. If there was a place to pitch a tent or park a camper, it was being used. The lake was now home to dozens of hard core druggies. Whatever you wanted to use to get high on, one of the campsites had it for sale. What was once a get away from it all lake, was now a very populated drug store.

I found out that I could get an extension on my unemployment benefits, so every two weeks when I picked up a check I invested it in drugs. I would literally buy drugs to sell drugs, to buy more drugs to sell more drugs, so that I could do more drugs. There was a time when I had to drive all around the county to find my drug of choice. Now, all I had to do is walk around the lake to do my shopping.

I didn't even have to leave the lake to find companionship. There was as many different kinds of girls as there where different kinds of drugs. There were short girls, tall girls, skinny girls, fat girls, old girls, young girls, pretty girls and ugly girls. They were on my shopping list too, but I was usually too drunk to care if she was a bargain or not. I can't tell you how many times I wanted to return the falsely advertised merchandise after I sobered up.

I went to town to pick up my check and try to score some weed to sell one morning. When I got back to the lake nothing was there, not a tent, camper or a person. The place looked as though a cleaning crew decided to make the place spotless. Even my tent had vanished. I went to the park to find out what had happened. I was told that the police had come and kicked everybody out. Some of the hard core campers moved to another campsite by a different lake. I went out to the new campsite, and I was not impressed. I had to cross a 20 ft. long mud hole by walking on 2x8 planks to get to it. The place had a few dry areas to pitch tents, but most of it was swamp. There was a lake about seventy-five yards from the campsite, but it was hidden by trees. It was like moving from a great neighborhood to the slums, but it would have to do for now.

I had promised my girlfriend, Gale that I would not get high for one whole day. She had been dating me for six months and had never seen me straight. About noon the day I was to keep this promises Ralphs' younger brother, David, came to see me. He asked me if I wanted to try a hit of LSD. I told him about the promise I had made to Gale. David said not to worry because the drug would wear off by the time I was to see her. I took the hit then I panicked. David was a prankster and he was always trying to get Gale mad at me. This time he would succeed.

David gave me a four way hit, which meant that it should be divided between four people. I had done a lot of paper acid but it was nothing compared to this. This acid was called Mr. Natural. Most acids start to work in about a half hour. It had been two hours since I had taken the hit and I could feel the drug working but it was weak. I had two more hours before I had to pick Gale up so I figured that I had it made. Man, was I off!

I had a small buzz going when I picked Gale up, but I was feeling the effect of the drug getting stronger during the ride out to the campsite. As we walked across the planks to the campsite, the mud started changing colors. I was getting the impression that I had been took. As the minutes passed, I started to worry. Things around me started changing shapes and glowing. I looked down at my legs and saw large blades of fluorescent grass glowing and growing and wrapping around my legs. This was not like any acid I had ever taken before. There was a huge glowing log rolling towards me and when I jumped everyone around me laughed and wondered what I was jumping for.

All of the people were glowing, and I was having a hard time finding my hands. I looked over towards the lake and I saw people out on the water, swimming and skiing and having fun. There was even a large sailboat on the water. Now, I knew that my tricking Gale into thinking that I was straight was going to be impossible. After all, I was in the middle of our campsite and you could not even see the lake from there.

I was freaking out. I asked Gale to take me for a walk to get me out of there. I had to hold on to her just to walk. Coming towards us was Reds mom and dad. Her dad was floating about six feet in the air and his mom's head did not have a body. Both of them were glowing wild colors as he flew and she rolled towards me. I think that they said hello, but I was not about to stop and find outt. The mud puddle looked like glowing Neapolitan ice cream now, so I skipped the bridge and walked through the beautiful glowing mud instead.

Gail and I walked to the top of a small hill and I looked across at the glowing fields, and the gorgeous blue sky. Gale looked at me and said, "Look Mike, God's coming". Clouds started racing everywhere. I remember thinking, please God not now. When I figured out that I was hallucinating I almost forgot that I loved Gail, and I wanted to kill her. I warned her to never do that again. We walked back to the camp and I had to find someone to take Gail home. She had a curfew and it was about that time. One of her girlfriends volunteered to drive there as long as I promised to drive back.

I promised, but I kept my word to do that just like I kept my word to Gail to stay straight. I could not even make out the road. The pavement had the pattern of a huge snake and it moved as we rode on it. So Gale's girlfriend had to drive back. It had been about ten hours since I took the acid, and now I was praying that I would come down. I promised God that I would never do acid again. This was one day with three broken promises. It was early morning when I finally started getting it together. The lights started fading and the fire started looking real. I thought to myself, never again.

David knew what he was doing. The night before David , Joe and a couple of girls spent the night in Joe's pop-up camper. They said that they watched a beautiful line move all around the canvas that covered the camper. When they woke up, the canvas had disappeared. Someone had touched a cigarette to the canvas and it burnt up while they watched. All four of them shared one hit.

I was twenty three and tired of being broke all of the time. So when my friend William suggested that we enlist in the army, I was game. Three weeks after William brought the idea up; I was on a plane headed to Ft. Jackson, South Carolina. I was going to finally make something out of myself.

CHAPTER FOUR

YOU'RE IN THE ARMY NOW

I never thought that I would be on a plane, especially a plane that was flying me to the army for Basic Training. I was half drunk when I boarded the plane, and they served alcohol during the flight. We would be landing about 2:00 AM. It was about 11:00 PM now. I had a fear of flying so; of course, I would need to drink to calm my nerves.

By the time we landed, I had drunk about four miniature bottles of whiskey. I went straight from the plane to a military bus filled with about twenty five other young men who looked lost. The next thing I knew we were getting off the bus and men with round brimmed hats were giving us orders. "Line up behind the yellow line. There is a yellow barrel in front of the doorway; this is your last chance to get rid of any illegal substances. If you have any weapons or drugs, put them in the barrel. Anything you put in the barrel now will not be charged against you. This is your one and only chance to get rid of your illegal paraphernalia or contraband."

As we entered the building, you could see lots of stuff being tossed into the barrel. We were taken to a small auditorium and we were asked to take a seat. There were a few of the men with the round hats in the room. We soon found out that they were drill sergeants, and we were to do everything that they told us to do. The introduction to the reception station did not take long. For the next three days we were going to get new clothes, new equipment, plenty of shots, and a new attitude.

As we left this room, we were given one more chance to get rid of anything illegal, and again I watched as stuff was tossed into the barrel. We were taken to a room with lots of bunk beds and warned that we would start our day early. It was about 3:00 AM now and my head was pounding. It seemed like minutes, but I got to sleep a whole three hours. My hangover lasted all morning. The pounding in my head lasted for three days. Those round hats must have been screwed on until they hurt. That is the only reason I could think of that would make the men wearing them scream that loud.

When my three days at the reception station were complete, I was ready to go to my unit where I would do my basic training. It had to be better than the last three days. I was wrong again. Basic training was identical to the reception station. Just another bunch of men with their round hats screwed on too tight.

Whenever I was in a situation that I knew that I could not handle alone, I went to the Lord for help. I made it through basic training without a drop of alcohol or any drugs. I would even read my Bible every day, and attend church on Sundays. I graduated from basic training and I had eight more weeks of A.I.T., "Advanced Individual Training", to complete before I would be sent to my permanent post at Ft. Campbell Kentucky.

By the time I graduated from A.I.T., four months had passed and I had not fallen to any of the temptations that haunted my life in the past. I was offered weed and I refused it; I was invited to go out drinking and said no. In one week, I was going to reconcile with my family and bring my son Jeremy with me to my permanent duty station at Ft. Campbell Kentucky.

Look, what the Lord had done. He took a twenty three years old drug addict, alcoholic, womanizing, dead beat-dad, out-of-shape bum, and turned him into a sober, respectable, man. I was proud of the person I had become. This would be my last weekend at Ft. Jackson. There were four men that went through basics and A.I.T. with me. They were going out for what was most likely going to be their last night of being together. They started begging me to go out with them. They promised that they would not try to talk me into drinking. I could not say no. After all, I would most likely never see them again. I was passed out in the back of the taxi when we got back to the barracks. I could only remember bits and pieces of the night out, but mostly just the parts where I made an ass of myself. I woke up the next morning hung over and ashamed. I should have studied the book of Proverbs and listened to the warnings. **Proverbs 26:11** "As a dog that returns to his **vomit**, So is a fool that repeats his folly."

On the flight to Texas, I got drunk again. I spent a week in Texas drinking and bragging that God was calling me to be a pastor. I figured that I would quit drinking again as soon as I got to Ft. Campbell. I should have known better. After all, how many times had I tried to serve the Lord before?

My first year and a half at Ft. Campbell was not even close to what it could have been. I could have been a good husband, good dad, and a good soldier. Instead I was terrible at all three.

I chased after strange woman, I did drugs and drank alcohol, and I played army just enough to get by. My brother came to stay with me, but on one of our nights out bar-hopping a person driving towards us with his headlights out, ran us off the road. I was drunk, so I turned the car around and I chased after him. He pulled into a driveway and ran behind a house. My brother was drunk, so he decided to chase after the man. That was a dumb move. Just a few moments after my brother ran out of my sight, he returned holding his chest. My brother was screaming for me to take him to a hospital. When my brother ran after the man, he stabbed him in his lung. I went speeding towards the main roads hoping that a policeman would see me and pull me over. There was no such thing as a cell phone back then. I saw a police car in a parking lot, and I pulled up next to him screaming for help.

The officer called for an ambulance for my brother. When they arrived, the officer took me to look for the man that stabbed him. We could not find the man. I did not know if my brother was going to live or die. He ended up pulling through. My parents drove down to see him at the hospital. As soon as he was released, he went back home with them. I know! You would think that almost losing my brother would snap me back to reality? It did not.

During my first year and a half in the army, my house was raided and the civilian police confiscated two marijuana plants and a tray of seeds. The army let the civilian courts handle that. I also got a drunk driving on post and lost my promotion from E2 to E3 for a few months. That cost me money. Also, I had to pay one hundred dollars a month for car insurance, which was a lot in 1979. That also cost me a lot of money. That was the easy stuff.

I got a phone call from my mother telling me that my niece, Renee, had died. She was only ten years old and she had battled cystic fibrosis all of her young life. I was told that right before her life ended that she smiled a huge smile and that she lifted her hands towards heaven and said "I'm going home". If anything was going to help soften the pain of losing a child, it would have to be watching her pass away with such peace.

The army said that they would let me have a leave of absence for five days and the Red Cross gave me money. I would only have enough cash for me to go, so my wife and son would have to stay home.

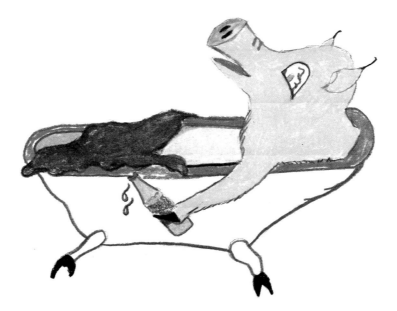

When I arrived home I went to my sister's house to let her know that I was there for her. I spent a whole two hours being there for her, then I had my mom drop me off at the bar so that I could visit old friends. I stayed at the bar getting drunk until closing. I did not have a ride back to my mother's house, so I ended up spending the night with a couple I was drinking with. They lived close to the bar. I woke up the next morning in their bathtub which was full of their dirty laundry. And it stunk! I deserved to wake up where I did. Again, I emphasize the Bible says in Proverbs 26:11 "As dog returns to his own vomit, so a fool repeats his folly". My head was pounding, and the smell was putrid.

I called my mother and had her come get me. She took me back to my sister's house so I could wash off the stench from the filthy cloths that I had an affair with. I was able to wash off the smell of the night's folly from the outside of my body, but the guilt that accompanied it would last a lifetime. When my sister said that she was going to the funeral home for visitation that afternoon, it was my chance to desert her again. I went back to the bar and got drunk again. This time when the bar closed I bought a couple of cases of beer and went with a group of friends to one of their homes and we partied most of the morning. This time, after a short cat nap, one of them gave me a ride back to my mother's home.

I had been in town three days and I had spent a total of six hours consoling my sister. This was the most devastating thing that could happen to a person in their lifetime, and I was still thinking only of me. I can't imagine the pain that she must have been going through, and I pray that I will never have to. At the funeral my sister tried to tell me how great Renee looked. She asked me to go look at her. Again, I just thought of myself, and I told her no, I want to remember her as she was.

Does everything I told you up to this point in my life disgust you? How do you like me now?

It was just a couple of months after that when my other sister's daughter, Christie, died. She was just one year old. I asked for another week of absence, but it was not granted. Today, when I think about the army rejecting my request for leave I consider it God's mercy. I already live with the guilt of my actions when Renee passed away. What kind of guilt would I have had to live with if the army would have granted my leave?

There was a man in my unit named Joe. I really liked Joe so after he had asked me to go to church with him several times I said, yes. My transformation from a life consumed with regrets to a life filled with meaning was lightning fast. In a few weeks, I was a regular at church, and within a couple of months I was driving the church bus picking up children for Sunday school. I was never happier. I started inviting friends of mine to go to church with me. Some of them saw the change in me and decided that they wanted whatever I had.

My faith was going to get tested after a few months of living for the Lord. My son Jeremy came home from school with a note from his teacher. The note said that I should take Jeremy to an eye doctor and get his eyes examined. He was having a hard time seeing the blackboard. Now, I was going to have to make a decision. Was I going to listen to the teacher or trust God for a healing? I decided to trust in the Lord.

Over the next few weeks I received more notes from Jeremy's teacher. The last one said that she had moved Jeremy to the front of the class, and he still could not read the blackboard. She also said that if I would not get Jeremy glasses, then I was not to send him to school.

If there is one thing that I know about God is that He has perfect timing. That week an evangelist known for his gifts in healing was going to be holding a service in a town close by. I can't tell you who invited me to the service or even how I got there, but what happened at the service I will never forget. After the praise and worship and a short sermon on faith the evangelist started praying for people.

Jeremy was sleeping so I carried him up front for prayer. The pastor put his hand on Jeremy's head and started praying for him. When the pastor finished praying for my son, I carried him back to my seat. The pastor was still praying for others when my son opened his eyes. I knew instantly that God had healed him because he was born with a wandering eye and both eyes were straight.

The next Monday I sent him back to school. I wondered all day what his teacher was going to say. When Jeremy got home, I asked him, "Well, what did your teacher say"? All he said was that he told her that God healed him. I never heard another word from his teacher.

I spent the rest of my enlistment in the military at Ft. Campbell. For the next year and a half I was a proud Christian husband, a proud Christian father, and a good Christian soldier. Now my time in the service was about to end.

I wanted to go home, but I was afraid. All of my life up to now I did not know if I was in a battle or not. This was different. This time I knew that whatever I decided was going to impact my life from then on. The recruiters let me know that if I reenlisted I would have to go to Korea for two years without my family. I also knew that there was a possibility that I might lose my family if I went home.

My old friends lived back home and I already knew from experience that I was weak when I was around them, but not seeing my family for two years might be worse. I tried to get the recruiters to sign papers that said if I reenlisted that I could stay with my family for my reenlistment tour. The recruiters said that they could not make that promise so I took my discharge. My time in the military was finished.

CHAPTER FIVE

BACK HOME WHAT SHOULD I DO?

I found a job as soon as I got back home and within a few weeks I was buying a house on a land contract. I don't know why I was so worried? All that I had to do now was find a church. I would leave the house on Sunday mornings with a church in mind, but there was always a reason for me not to go in. The parking lot was too full or they might not be affiliated with the church that I went to when I was in the army, or any number of other reasons. Whatever the reason, my biggest fear was about to happen and I had no support from a church family to encourage me or guide me.

Red came to see me a couple of times a week. When she did, she would usually want me to go for a ride with her so that she could get high. The first time that she did this she respectfully asked me if smoking a joint in front of me would bother me, and, of course, I said no. Partially, because I figured that she was an adult, and what she did was up to her, and partially because I knew that if I smoked one joint that I would want to smoke a cigarette also.

A couple of months had passed and I still had not found a local church that I liked. It was Mid-September and the salmon were getting ready to start their annual run. Every autumn the Salmon would swim out of Lake Michigan and swim up shallow creeks that flowed into it to spawn, and every year I would be waiting for them with my spear in hand. It was against the law, but I figured that God put them there to eat so there was nothing wrong with me taking a few.

Dan had never gone salmon spearing so I talked him into going down to the creek with me to spear a couple. I had a spot back in the woods where we could wait for the fish to swim by. We were hidden well enough so that the DNR could not see us. Dan smoked cigarettes, and the smell of them was really tempting me. Whenever I used to hunt or fish, I always smoked to keep from getting bored while I waited for my prey. I stupidly figured what would be the harm in smoking just one?

I should have been paying better attention. I was not going to church, I stopped reading the Bible, and my prayer life was sporadic. This fishing trip was not a coincidence. The devil set his trap skillfully. First, he tempted me with something he knew I loved doing. Then he tempted me with doing something I always did while I waited for fish to swim by.

Dan and I left the creek with three salmon. Besides them, I came back home with something else that I did not have when I left. I was now having an irresistible urge to smoke. Even though it had been almost two years since I took a puff that was all it took to start my addiction again.

This was just the first part of the devil's plan to stop me from telling people about Jesus .Satan's plan was to corrupt my mind more than he already did. Now he had to finish his work and destroy me. Red stopped by for another visit and we went for another ride.

This time when she fired up a joint I asked her for a hit. She tried to talk me out of it, but I could tell that she was not sincere. The devil's plan worked. He tempted me with compromise and finished me with outright disobedience.

Only a few weeks had passed since my trip to the creek, and I was already planning my twenty seventh birthday party at my home. When I got out of the army in August, I was driving kids to church every Sunday morning. I had not smoked a cigarette, drank any alcohol or done any drugs in a year and a half. This was only two months later, and I was already destroying everything that God had done for me. Was I really this stupid, and uncaring? Or was my enemy craftier than I gave him credit for? Whatever the reason was, I was caught in his trap again, and this time he was going to make sure I stayed there.
If you were to examine my life you could watch my evolution of destruction.

Matthew 12:43-45 "when the unclean spirit is gone out of a man, he walks through dry places, seeking rest, and finds none. Then he says I will return into my house from whence I came out; and when he is come, he finds it empty, swept, and garnished. Then goes he, and takes with himself seven other spirits more wicked than himself, and they enter in and dwell there: and the last state of that man is worse than the first. Even so shall it be also unto this wicked generation."

Paul said it right in Romans 7:15-25

Romans 7:15-25[15] "For that which I do I know not: for not what I would, that do I practice; but what I hate, that I do.[16] But if what I would not, that I do, I consent unto the law that it is good.[17] So now it is no more I that do it, but sin which dwelled in me.[18] For I know that in me, that is, in my flesh, dwelled no good thing: for to will is present with me, but to do that which is good is not.[19] For the good which I would I do not: but the evil which I would not, that I practise.[20] But if what I would not, that I do, it is no more I that do it, but sin which dwelled in me.[21] I find then the law, that, to me who would do good, evil is present.[22] For I delight in the law of God after the inward man:[23] but I see a different law in my members, warring against the law of my mind, and bringing me into captivity under the law of sin which is in my members.[24] Wretched man that I am! who shall deliver me out of the body of this death?[25] I thank God through Jesus Christ our Lord. So then I of myself with the mind, indeed, serve the law of God; but with the flesh the law of sin. "

I have to ask myself how? How did I let myself leave a life of fulfillment with God, and enter into a life of turmoil? Why? Why would I take a chance on losing everything I have? Did I think that I could enter the enemy's camp just a little and still serve God? The bible said in **Revelation 3:16** "So because thou art **lukewarm**, and neither hot nor cold, I will spew thee out of my mouth.

I got high every day, I got drunk every weekend, and I neglected my responsibilities as a husband and father. Everything was gradual at first and I thought that I had everything under control. When I was serving God, I would pray for a hedge of protection around me and my family. Now I quit praying and the enemy walked right in.

Let me show you how that worked. When I was serving the Lord, most of my old friends avoided me. I was not doing drugs, so I was not being introduced to drug dealers. I was content with my wife, so I stayed away from other woman. I stayed sober, so I was not seduced by immorality. I did not go to parties so my children did not need to have babysitters and they spent time with me. The closer I got to God, the farther away from sin I was.

This worked vice versa. I gradually forced God out of my life and I invited the devil in. Within a few short years I lost everything God had given me. I lost my family, and dived deeper than I had ever gone into a pit of immorality.

Let me do a quick summary of my life up to now. I wanted to get drunk and Oscar got killed. I wanted to go to a dance and ended up getting drunk and went to jail; I got drunk again and went to jail again; I got drunk again and went to jail again. I got drunk again and ended up at the hospital with carbon monoxide poisoning, I got drunk with Lee and he was murdered; I got high with Butch and he murdered his girlfriend; I got high with Walt and he committed suicide; I got drunk with my brother and he got stabbed. To top it all off, I got high and deserted my whole family.

Did I miss something? I can't explain what I do not understand. I cry when I think about the past, but what can I do? I can't change it.

CHAPTER SIX

THIRTY HOW DID I GET HERE?

If somebody was to ask me what I would be doing when I reached thirty, I would have said: "You have got to be joking; I will never make it to thirty." Fooled me! I'm still here.

I got my old job back with my friend Joe. And we went right back to where we left off. We would do a job, get paid, get drunk, then do another job. Joe was married now and he had two young daughters and a baby son. Joe and his wife were both alcoholics. I don't know how they managed a family, but they did. Even though Joe's lifestyle did not resemble that of a Christian man, I don't think a day went by that he did not mention Jesus or pray.

Joe was born to be a roofer. He weighed about 120 lbs. and he was fast. He could hand nail shingles just about as fast as a man with a nail gun. Joe would stick to a roof like a fly to a wall. I watched him do some wild stuff on the jobs. One day it was really windy and Joe needed me to hand him up a sheet of plywood. I handed the sheet to Joe, and Joe lifted it up over his head. The wind caught the plywood, and I watched Joe fly off from the roof and the plywood acted just like a parachute. Joe didn't skip a beat. The minute his feet hit the ground he walked over to the ladder and he carried the plywood back up to the roof himself.

When Joe was on the roof, he had the ability to avoid mishaps that would cause most roofers serious injury. But when Joe was finished working for the day and started drinking he would lose his ability to avoid accidents.

Joe had a lot of accidents driving drunk, and it was only by the grace of God that it was usually just the car that got damaged and nobody got hurt. Joe did not let an accident stop him from driving for long. There was always someone that would let him use their vehicle. I got to Joe's house to pick him up for work one morning, and he told me that I would have to find other work for a couple of months. He said that he was going to sign himself into rehab.

Joe had borrowed his dad's truck and got drunk while he was driving it. The truck was a classic but his dad had it insured with minimal coverage. Joe totaled out the truck and felt terrible because he could not afford to get his dad another one. He knew that his dad could not afford another one either.

While Joe was at rehab, I would have to find another way to support myself. I had a friend named Trapper who always had some scam going to make money. When I met Trapper, he was making money selling tickets to a rodeo that he was promoting in his back yard. The Rodeo consisted of one horse and a few drunks who thought that they were cowboys. They could not even climb on the horse while someone was holding it still. They were having a hard enough time sitting on a bale of hay without falling off. Nobody wanted their money returned to them because the band was great and the beer was included in the price.

Trapper's friend had given him a few pounds of weed to sell, but Trapper did not have the buyers to sell the weed. Trapper asked me if I could sell some of the weed for him because he knew that most of my friends were drug addicts. This would work out great.

Paul and Pattie were my two best customers. I had partied with these two for years. I could count on them to buy a couple of ounces a week. These two spent every weekend and most weekdays looking for a party. They must have invented the phrase bar-hopping. They would go wherever the party was. One evening while they were at my house to buy some pot Pattie told me this story.

My brother has a pilot's license and a small airplane. He knows that I am afraid of heights but he still tries to talk me into flying with him. Yesterday, I said ok, but only if he promised not to ask me again. Everything was going fine until he decided to try and scare me. We were flying low and he said that he was going to fly the plane underneath the walkway bridge that crossed the road below us. He scared me to death when he did it. I thought for sure that I was going to die. I will never fly with him again.

I know where the bridge was located and Pattie's brother would have hit phone lines or some other wires if he actually flew under the bridge. Pattie must have covered her eyes as her brother took the airplane down. Either way, I heard that he lost his pilot's license.

The next day I got the news. Paul and Pattie went off the road and hit a tree while they were riding around partying. Pattie was killed, and Paul was in the hospital severely injured.

Pattie's death in the accident did not stop anybody from drinking or driving drunk. Paul was in the hospital for months, but when he was discharged he was right back to his old habit of bar-hopping and partying. The only thing that changed was that his hop was now a limp.

Joe came out of rehab a new man. He partnered up with his friend Max who he had trained a couple of years earlier. Max didn't do drugs, and he only drank once in a great while. These two would be the dream team of roofers. Every time these two got on a roof it would become a race to see who could lay the most shingles. They worked me hard, but they paid me good. I had never seen Joe this intense about his work before.

One day Joe and Max watched a crew of roofers break for lunch. For a joke, they hopped on the roof and finished it before the crew returned. Joe and Max didn't even stick around to see how the other roofers reacted. I could just imagine what went through their minds when they returned.

Whenever Joe got a day off from work, he went fishing. He lived for rainy days when he could not work. The weather might keep him from doing a job, but it was not going to stop him from fishing. Besides, everyone knows that fish bite better in the rain.

Joe's transformation from a unpredictable alcoholic to a dependable father, partner and friend was amazing. There were times when Joe drank, that you could not stand to be around him. Now Joe was a changed man. He was actually a man that all of us looked up to.

A couple of months had passed since Joe quit drinking, and I did not want to be a cause of him losing his sobriety. Trapper and I were going to go to the river after work on Friday and do some catfish fishing. Trapper started every morning with a pint of whiskey, and then he drank beer for the rest of the day. I was friends with Trapper for a long time, and I never saw a day pass where he didn't drink.

Joe found out what Trapper and I had planned, and there was no way that he was going to let us go fishing without him. I told Joe that we were going to be drinking and that he would not be able to resist the temptation to drink. Joe would not have it. He was going fishing, and he was going to stay sober and that was that.

Before we left for the river, I took a hit of acid. I used acid like most people used speed. It helped me to stay awake and function while I was drinking. I asked Trapper if he wanted one. Trapper could not say no. Trapper's whole life was spent bragging on how well that he could hunt, fish, and trap. He had to train the best dogs, catch the biggest fish, and harvest the most furs. He also loved it when he could tease me about anything that I did that was dumb or foolish. Giving him a hit of acid was just my way of getting even. Trapper was an alcoholic; he was not a drug addict.

On the way to the river, we had to stop and get supplies. Trapper was starting to feel the effects of the acid, and he was afraid to get out of the car and go into the store. He gave me some money to help buy a couple of cases of beer and cigarettes.

When I came out of the store, Trapper jumped into the back seat with the beer and Joe got up front with me. When we got to the river Trapper was feeling the full effect of the acid. By the time Joe and I got our fishing poles and gear out of the trunk, Trapper had disappeared. I found him underneath the bridge hiding. He was afraid that someone was going to see him. We were parked off from the main road, we had not seen any other vehicles, and there was no one else around.

I decided to give Trapper a break and told him to get back in the car and I would take him to a different fishing spot. We kept on drinking while we drove to a spot ten miles away. Beer would work as a downer and, hopefully, it would take the edge off the acid before we got to the next spot. We got to the new location and Trapper said that he was going to walk down the creek bank to find a good spot to fish.

Joe and I finished getting the rest of our gear out of the trunk and we hauled it down the side of the hill next to the bridge we had parked on. We cast our baits into the water, and I told Joe that I would go find Trapper. When I found Trapper, he was on his knees with a hook in one hand and a worm in the other. He looked at me like he was about ready to cry. He said that he could not get the worm on the hook and asked me if I would do it for him.

I told Trapper to grab his stuff, and we went back to get Joe so that we could drive to another fishing hole. The next spot was about a half hour drive from where we were, and I was sure that Trapper would have his act together before we got there. Now, I had another problem, when we got back to Joe, Joe had a beer in his hand. You would be surprised how fast a person can get drunk after they quit drinking for a couple of months. When we got to our next spot, we had to carry our gear a couple of hundred yards to the river. There was a dirt road going back to the spot where we were going to fish, but the company that owned the land put a cable across the road so that no one could drive back to the river. They didn't care if you fished on their property. They didn't even care if you parked in their parking lot. They just did not want you to drive your vehicle on their land.

Trapper was coming down off from his acid trip and Joe was still able to walk so we grabbed the case of beer that was left, our fishing gear and walked back to spot where we were going to fish. Finally! We stayed there until we ran out of beer. We started packing everything up to carry back to the car when Joe decided that would be too much work. He was going to go get the car and drive it back to us.

When Joe got back, we loaded up the car and I took over driving. Guards stopped me as soon as I got close to where the cable had crossed the road. I don't know how Joe knocked the cable down but it was now lying on the ground. The guards gave us a good chewing out and warned us that if we ever came back that they would call the police.

That night was one that I will never forget. Trapper lost all of his bragging rights, Joe lost his sobriety, and I had one more memory that I would like to forget.

When Joe started drinking, Max quit the partnership. Max knew that he couldn't count on Joe to carry his half of the work load anymore, so it was time for him to move on. I stayed working with Joe. If Joe got too drunk to work, who cared? I usually had a hangover too.

It was just a short time after Joe started drinking again that Joe decided to get some much needed dental work done. He needed his teeth pulled, and he told his dentist to yank them all on the same day. The dentist didn't want to do it, but it was the only way that Joe was going to get the surgery done. The state was going to pay for it so the dentist said ok.

Joe was in terrible pain, and this was a good excuse to get drunk. We went to a tavern that was a few miles from my house, because they had a live band playing instead of just a juke box. His brother, Mark, said that he would drive. We drank until the bar closed then we went to another friend's house with a bunch of other people to drink some more and snort a little cocaine. I had tried just about every drug that was ever made, but I had never had the opportunity to sample cocaine. I was not impressed.

I told you that Joe was a small man, and when he got drunk he had a big mouth. Physically he had a tiny mouth. His brother Mark on the other hand, was a quiet person with a big mouth.Mark. Mark had false teeth and Joe decided that he wanted to put Mark's teeth in his mouth to see what he would look like. We all got to see the Cheshire cat in person.

We partied for a couple more hours, and Mark took me home. After he dropped me off, he took Joe home and dropped him off. I went to the bar the next evening by myself, and the waitress told me that she thought that Joe had AIDS. She was telling people at the bar how Joe was spitting into his glass and how skinny he was. I told her that Joe chewed tobacco, and he was always spitting it into glasses and he was always skinny.

A day or two later, Joe and his wife came out to my house very early in the morning. They were both drinking beer and starting to get drunk. I told Joe what the waitress was saying about him and he got mad and decided to go to the bar and confront her. Joe wasn't gone long. The waitress had not started her shift yet, so Joe came back with a twelve pack of beer to drink while he waited. When the beer was gone, Mark and his wife went back to the bar. I don't know what happened after that. I heard that he argued with the waitress, and he was mad when he left the place. I got a call from his brother a couple of hours after Joe had left my house. He told me that Joe had gotten into an accident. He said that the hospital called and they wanted him to come there.

The hospital was not permitted to tell Joe's brother that Joe was killed in the accident until a coroner pronounced him dead. Joe's wife lived through the accident, but she damaged both of her legs. Now, Joe's wife would not have a husband and his children would not have a dad. How much of this insanity would I have to experience before I had enough? How many more tragedies would I live through before the victim was me?

It was not long after that, I was at the bar with Max and his girlfriend Jill waiting on her brother Mike to meet us there. Mike never came. Mike was drunk and hit a tree on his way to meet us. He died instantly. I had close calls when I was driving drunk, but I always seemed to narrowly escape injury. I went to a tavern out of town one time just to get away. The road that I had to travel was full of curves. As I was driving home, I lost control of my car while coming around one of those sharp corners and I drove my car over the hill on the opposite side of the road. The hill was steep and a long way down. My car went past a lot of trees but it never hit any of them. When the car came to a stop, there were trees on both sides of it. A few inches to the right or left and I might not be telling this story.

Then there was the time that I took a girlfriend out dancing. It was winter and the parking lot at the bar was icy. When we decided to leave, I was drunk. I tried to squeeze by a van's front bumper and dented in the side of my car. When I did that, I got mad and threw the car in reverse and I backed into a parked truck that had a high iron pipe bumper that smashed my tail light out when I hit it. Then I hit one more car on my way out of the parking lot. At least, Ralph just hit trees.

There was another night when I left the bar drunk that I missed the curve completely. I was not in a ditch, but I could not get the car to move. I finally got mad, gave up and I left the car there. The next morning I had a friend take me to get my car, and there was a police officer standing next to it. At first, I told my girlfriend to keep on driving, but I decided to face up to the accident. The police officer told me that I was lucky that he did not catch me the night before. I looked at the spot where my car came to a stop.

The reason that I could not get it to move was because there was a huge branch pinning the car in between it and the ground. A few feet in front of the car stood a chain link fence that had a sign that read cemetery. How many warnings would I get? And why was I still alive?

CHAPTER SEVEN

LORDY, LORDY ALMOST FORTY

Life has a lot of twist and turns. How and why things happen I cannot explain, but it is a small world after all. Do you remember my friend Ralph? He was the prize fighter who beat up his Toyota. Ralph ended up riding a motorcycle instead of driving a car. Ralph was a heavy drinker and I guess that we all knew that it would be just a matter of time before he got in trouble. Ralph was riding his motorcycle on a country road one evening. Of course, he had been drinking. There were a couple of guys at the end of a driveway on the same road Ralph was traveling. They were getting ready to pull out onto the road. The guys in the car were also drinking. They did not see Ralph, and Ralph did not see them. They pulled out of the drive, and Ralph smashed into the side of their car. Ralph died on impact.

My friend who drove me to get my car from its parking place at the cemetery was Sam's cousin. He was the guy that Ralph said sucker punched him, so Ralph went back and hit Sam's fist with his other eye. Well, Sam was married now to a girl named Ronda. One day, when I went over to my friend's house, Sam and Ronda were there visiting. We had a few beers together and we all decided to go to the tavern and shoot some pool.

After a couple of hours of drinking, Sam started getting belligerent. Ronda came over to me and asked me if I could help her get Sam out of the bar before a fight broke out. Sam was in an argument with someone he was shooting pool with and he wanted to fight. It took a little bit of coaxing, but I finally talked Sam into leaving. I have been around a lot of people like Sam in my life. If you want to fight, just add alcohol. This would be my first and last time drinking around Sam. I liked the bar where we were drinking, and I did not want to be asked to leave permanently because of some other person's personality. I had enough problems with my own. A little while after that night, I was in the same bar shooting pool with another friend named Dave. We had been drinking for a couple of hours when Steve showed up and joined us. Steve was my hot rod friend that worked on cars in his mother's garage. Over the years Steve and I became good friends. The three of us took turns ordering shots of whiskey to drink with our beers. The bar was dead that night; except for a couple of regulars, the place was empty.

We decided that we would go to another bar that was five miles down the road and see if we could find some action there. Steve said that he would beat us there; so the race was on. Dave and I ran to my car. We knew that Steve liked speeding, and that the only way we were going to beat him was with a head start.

Dave and I won the race and stayed at this bar until closing, but Steve never showed up. Dave and I just figured that he must have found something more interesting to do, or, maybe, he just went home. Who knows? After the bar closed Dave spent the night at my house.

My head was pounding when Dave came into my bedroom and woke me up. He said that he needed to get home. About half way back to Dave's house, we rounded a curve and a police officer flagged us down to stop. There were all kinds of emergency vehicles behind him. There was just one lane in the gravel to the left of the cluster, and we needed to wait until the traffic cleared from the opposite direction before we could proceed. As soon as he could, the officer waved us through.

Dave and I tried to look to see if we could see any cars that we recognized, but our vision was blocked. We knew somebody was in an accident, but we did not know who. I continued driving Dave home and when I dropped him off I told him to call me if he found out anything about the accident.

I had to pass by the accident on my way back home, but I still could not see anything. The area was still packed with emergency vehicles. I went back home and went back to bed.

A couple of hours later my sleep was interrupted again. Dave was on the other end of the line. Dave told me that the reason Steve never showed up at the bar was because he was killed in the accident that we passed that morning. Steve was dead. I told Dave that I was coming to get him so that we could look at the place where Steve died. We could not tell what caused the accident but we could see the route Steve's car traveled.

A creek flowed underneath the road and there were guard rails on both sides of the road. On the opposite side of the road in the direction Steve was coming from was a two-track drive way and a small parking spot for fisherman behind the guardrail. At the end of the parking spot was a small hill that was covered with cedar trees. The hill ended at the bank of the creek. From what Dave and I could tell, Steve crossed the road and went behind the guard rail. He drove on the two-track and through the small parking spot. He broke through the tops of the cedars and flew across the creek and landed on the opposite bank. Steve must have been traveling at a high speed to fly across the creek like that.

We would miss Steve but that was the only effect that the accident had on any of us. Nobody that I knew quit drinking after Steve died. Life goes on and so does the insanity.

Over the next few years, I lived with friends, girlfriends, and anybody who would let me stay with them. I worked on roofs in the summer months, and in the winter months I would sell drugs for money. Sometimes I let my friends support me. Randy was one of those friends.

Randy let me live with him for two years. Randy had cerebral palsy, and he was confined to a wheel chair. That did not stop him from partying though. Randy had a ton of friends and his house was a popular partying spot. Randy had a large three bedroom house and he let our friend Hank live in one of them and me in the other.

Hank was a big boy. He was over six feet tall and over three hundred pounds. When he was drinking and doing drugs, he did them to the best of his ability. There were a lot of times that he would have enough of that lifestyle and he would start going to church. For the next couple of months, he would try to get everyone he knew to repent, quit taking drugs, and go to church with him. About the time he would have you convince to go with him, he would be back to drinking and doing drugs. He was in the same boat that I was in, he just changed directions faster.

Hanks friend asked him one time, "What is it going to take to get you to serve the Lord? Are you going to have to be hit by a train?" A couple of weeks later he was sitting in his car at a stop sign waiting for traffic to clear. He was stopped on the railroad tracks. A train was coming at him blowing its whistle but Hank could not hear it because he had his music blasting so loud. The train hit him and wrecked his car, but Hank came out of it unharmed. We both knew that the accident was a warning, but for some reason it was just not loud enough.

I was going to go to a blue grass festival. This was an annual festival where I could get away with a group of friends and party for three days straight. I could also make some money selling drugs. The day that I was leaving to go to the festival, I stopped at a friend's house to get some drugs from him to sell. When I went inside his house, there were a bunch of people partying. I wasn't surprised by that, what I was not expecting to see were two very young teenage kids sitting on the floor in front of a coffee table. What they were wearing surprised me most. The boy was dressed in a dress shirt and pants and the girl was wearing a beautiful dress. They looked like they were going to go to a school prom or maybe a wedding. The rest of the people in the house were dressed in leather jackets and blue jeans. I picked up the drugs, but as I was leaving I could not help but think about those two kids.

Were they going to be safe? Should I see what they were doing there? Should I talk them into leaving? I decided to leave the situation alone and mind my own business. Whatever happened: happened. I went to the festival, but while I was there I could not get those teens out of my mind. When I got back to town, the first thing I heard about was those two kids. It was not them that I should have been worried about; it was the rest of the people at the party. The two teens left that party, and they went to an old man's house and brutally murdered him. They were into witchcraft, and they believed that the more he screamed the more power they got.

Would they have done this horrific murder if they were not high? I don't know. The drug that I had picked up to sell was paper acid. Did these two kids take that before they committed this murder? If they did, who sold it to them? I'm glad that I was not there. I had enough stuff on my conscience.

A person selling drugs doesn't know if the person that they are selling it to can handle it. What if the person buying the drug never took any drugs before? What if their system is not capable of digesting the drug? Not everybody reacts to a drug in the same way. A drug that makes one person laugh can make the next person depressed or paranoid. The people selling the drugs may not want to admit it, but, YES, you are responsible if something bad happens.

The guy that I was selling weed and acid for introduced me to a guy who was selling cocaine. Up to this point in my life, I never admitted or even thought that I was a drug addict or an alcoholic. I didn't even think that I could get addicted to a drug. Cocaine was going to prove me wrong.

The person letting me sell cocaine for him would set out a hundred dollars' worth of cocaine for us to do every time he dropped some off. When I started selling, I was just trying to get enough money to buy my own cigarettes so I did not have to bum from Randy. Pretty soon, I was selling cocaine so that I could pay for my own cocaine addiction.

The way that I looked at things was that if I could go a week or two without alcohol and it really did not bother me, then I must not be an alcoholic. I looked at drugs the same way. After all, I knew what an addiction felt like because I was addicted to smoking cigarettes.

Cocaine took me by surprise. I thought that it was just a nice high at first, and then I noticed that when I ran out I needed more. The chase was on. No matter how much cocaine I had it was never enough. There were times when I would go through hundreds of dollars' worth before I ran out, but the end result was always the same.

I never had anything take hold of me like this drug did. So much for me not getting addicted to anything! Every minute of every day turned out to be a quest for me. I had to get money somewhere so that I could get some cocaine. Selling cocaine was the only way that I could ever support my addiction.

I had to stop selling cocaine because the person who was letting me sell for him could not pay for his cocaine addiction. The person he was getting his drugs from was having the same problem. Most people cannot sell and use cocaine at the same time, and not get into trouble. I watched a lot of people lose everything they owned because of this drug.

One friend just finished building a log house and lost that to cocaine. Another friend lost his motor home, and another friend lost everything he owned. I was fortunate in a way; I did not have any material things to lose. It took a long time to escape the bondage that this drug had on me and it was not because I wanted to. The best way to escape any addiction is to be put in a position where you cannot get it. I was lucky, I had no drugs to sell and it was winter. No work, no money, meant no drugs.

I was almost forty when I moved out of Randy's house. It was spring and jobs were plentiful. I was able to buy a house on land contract. I decided to have a house warming party and, of course, I invited Randy. The party was a wild one. There was whiskey, beer, weed, and other drugs. Randy liked the hard liquor. I ended up passing out, and when I got up the next morning my living room was still full of people who had passed out wherever they could find a spot. Randy had his spot at the end of the couch.

After a night of drinking, all that Randy wanted was a chug of milk. I grabbed a jug, and he chugged down as much as he could. This was not unusual. Randy chugged milk even if he wasn't drinking. I went to the bathroom to clean up a little when another friend started beating on the door. He was yelling for me to hurry up because Randy was getting sick. I ran out to get Randy, and I wrapped my arms around his chest to lift him up so I could put him in his chair.

My face was just inches from his face. Randy's hands could not cover his mouth very well because of the cerebral palsy; It was like trying to stop water from leaking through a strainer. When I saw that he was about to throw up, I opened my mouth in shock. Randy was vomiting with such force that the curdled milk was shooting threw his hands into my open mouth with such force that I was swallowing as fast as Randy was spraying. All of the people in the room witnessing this unbelievable eruption of horrid smelling liquid started vomiting themselves. The room was emptied immediately. I cleaned what I could before taking Randy home. The only thing he was worried about was if I would invite him again.

A few weeks later I was out drinking and driving with another friend. We started arguing. I quit paying attention to my driving, and I drove off the side of a bridge and into the creek below. The water was only a foot or two deep so we got out of the car and climbed up the bank to the road. We were only a few blocks from her house, so we left the car and walked there.

We kept on drinking for a while at her house and my mouth started to hurt. I looked into a mirror and I saw what was causing the pain. The tip of my tongue was holding on with two small pieces of skin. There was one on each side of the hole that I made when I bit through my tongue. That really hurt, but I found out later that I broke my tailbone. That was really painful.

Let me do another quick summary of my life up to now. IT SUCKED!

CHAPTER EIGHT

HELP

When I was forty two, I moved out of Michigan and I moved to Grunge, Georgia. I started a roofing company with my friend Jack. We ran the business out of an apartment that we rented together. As much as I would like to stop right here and say that this was a good move, I can't.

When we first started the company, we kept our heavy partying for weekends. Jack and I both started to get ahead. New furniture was the first noticeable change. Within a few months, we went from throwing our roofing scrap into the back of a van to actually having a dump truck to toss it into.

Now that I was making some money, it was also time to invest in a higher quality of partying material. You guessed it. There is a lot of cocaine in Atlanta, and with the cocaine came a more expensive lifestyle. There were young girls who knew how to get you to support their addictions, and friends who wanted you to support them. Just like Randy had supported me.

It did not take long for our lives of imaginary luxury to dive into its' poor house reality. One Friday afternoon three families put their money together and gave Richard and me about four thousand dollars down payment so we could purchase material for their new roofs. We had good intentions but that did not do us a bit of good.
We went straight to our suppliers. First, our roofing supply store to pay for enough material to do one of the three houses. Then we went to our cocaine supplier to purchase a large quantity of drugs. We thought that we had everything under control. Material and drugs both paid for. What could possibly go wrong? Running out of cocaine before we were done partying was the beginning of what could go wrong.

We had to do something fast. We had a lot of money, but it was not ours. We were also craving more cocaine. The solution was easy. Since each home owner gave us half down for materials before we started their roofs, we would complete the first roof and get our pay when we finished. Then, we could buy material for the second roof out of that. So we took some of the money that we had and went and bought more cocaine.

There was one major flaw in our plan. What happens when you run out of drugs again? That was simple. You use the same logic that you used the first time you ran out of cocaine. You get more with all of the money that you have left. By Sunday afternoon we had spent thousands of dollars. Reality started settling in. I went to my bedroom and cried. Not because I spent all the money, but because I was out of cocaine.

My mother always knew when I was in trouble. Whenever she wanted to hear from me she would pray and within a few hours I would call her. This was not a onetime coincidence, this happened every time she prayed. She told me to start watching an evangelist on TV, and for me to start praying. I did what she asked, I really wanted to quit using drugs, but it seemed impossible. I managed to keep my weekday's drug free but I always lost the battle on weekends. By the way, I finally realize that I am in a battle.

Jack decided to move out and start a business by himself and I contacted my son and asked him to come down and work with me. I stayed away from the cocaine while he was here, but after a few weeks we had fallout and he left. Now I was alone.

I knew in my own mind that I would have to lose everything before I would quit abusing myself and return to the Lord. I started pawning and selling the things that I had without any way to get them back. Within a couple of months, I had nothing but my truck. I moved out of my apartment, and I moved into a crack house. The first month went great. I had money enough to purchase crack a couple of times a week, so the owner of the house treated me good. I still had my truck so I was still able to work. This was not part of God's plan. After about a month, my truck broke down. It needed a complete engine overhaul. The repair would cost me over a thousand dollars. There was no way I was going to be able to get it repaired.

I could not work so I had to do something to occupy my time. There were a few crossword puzzle books in the house so I started working on them. I can't tell you how it happened but within days I was designing my own crossword puzzles from books of the Bible.

I finally had enough pain in my life to make me quit drugs. Now, I was going to have to prove it. I found out quickly that the man that had the house let me stay so I could help buy drugs. When he saw that I had quit, the friendship that I thought that we had was over. I had no money and no place to go, so I stayed there and I let the puzzles consume me.

People would come in the house to smoke crack, but the Lord was keeping me strong. I was not offered anything and I was not asking for anything. The man who had the house would get mad at his girlfriend when she did not have money for him, and he would hit her. He left the house about seven o'clock every evening and he would return about ten. I finally got tired of watching him abuse his girlfriend and, I decided that I would put a stop to it. He left the house at his usual time, and I made a phone call to my mother. I let her know that I would not be able to call her after tonight because I was going to kill a man. I explained what had been happening, and that is all that I remember from the conversation.

I waited for the man to come home, but he never came back that night. The Lord had a different plan. The next day my mother wired me some money for a bus ticket home. I had a cousin that lived in Atlanta, and I called him to let him know that I was leaving. He said that he was going to Michigan in a few days and that I could stay with him and ride home for free.

He picked me up, and I stayed with him until he was ready to leave. I was forty two years old, and all that I owned was a suit case. When I got back home, my mother let me stay with her, but after a few days my sister let me stay in her spare bedroom.

I was so ashamed of myself that I could not face anyone. My best friend's wife committed suicide and I could not even get myself to go to her funeral because of shame and guilt. I didn't want anyone to see me broke and homeless.

I spent months trying to build a relationship with the Lord, but this book is not about that. This book is written to try and let the reader know that you are in a battle.

My friend Chip married the beautiful girl he was with when we worked at the celery farm. Through the years I watched as he transformed from a drinker and pot smoker, to a drug addict who had to sell drugs to pay for his own addictions. His beautiful wife caught him with another woman, and she left him and moved to California. When Chip found out where she went, he went after her. When he saw her, he told her how sorry he was and that if she came back to him that he would never be unfaithful again. She told him that she would come, back but if she ever caught him with another woman again she would leave and never come back. Chip kept on selling drugs, and it was not long that his wife caught him with another woman. Chip knew that she was going to leave him again so he hung himself.

Ralphs younger sister Tonya was never a violent person. She liked to drink beer and smoke weed. You would think that when her brother got killed in a motorcycle accident that she might stop getting high. It does not work that way. Usually, a person who has an addiction uses that addiction to help them through hard times. It is a quick fix for the moment but, sooner or later, you have got to face reality. Sometimes the quick fix destroys you. That's what happened to Tonya. Her boyfriend broke up with her so she got drunk to cover up the pain. Now, not only was she hurting, she was also not thinking. she put a gun to her head and took her own life.

I know how Tonya's mind was working, because I had been there many times. A girl that I loved would break up with me, and I would use my addictions to try to ease the pain. That never worked. It just made the situation worse. I would have killed myself many times if it was not for my Christian upbringing. I was afraid that if I killed myself, I would go to Hell. One of the main reasons you want to kill yourself is not because you are hurting, it's because you want to hurt the person who hurt you. It will not happen. All you did was stop any chance of reconciling with the person who left you. Now that you are gone, the person you killed yourself for now needs comforting. Where do you think they are going to go?

Sam and Ronda got a divorce, And Sam remarried, Sam never quit drinking, and he still could not control his temper. One night while he was drunk and arguing with his wife, he grabbed a gun and shot her. After he shot and killed her, he shot and killed himself. Their kids found them the next day. Do you think that Sam would have done this sober? I really do not think so.

Reds younger sister Brenda, who I partied with a lot through the years sat by a fire one night and told people that were sitting there with her exactly how she was going to kill herself. That did not surprise me at all. I never saw Brenda when she was not drinking, and it always seemed like she was hurting somebody. Her relationships always ended badly, and she hurt people that tried to help her. Sound like somebody else? I know how she felt. You wake up one day alone and depressed wondering what you have to live for. Brenda went back to the camper, and she turned on the gas. She committed suicide exactly the way that she said she would.

Trapper was a friend that I could write a book about. Some of the stories would be comical, and others would be heartbreaking or disgusting. Most of them would make you wonder. Like the time one winter that I took Ronda with me to visit Trapper. Trapper's dog was lying on the steps going into his house. Ronda reached down and patted the dog on the head on the way in. A few days later we went to visit Trapper again. The dog was in the same spot. Ronda reached done and patted the dog on the head again. A few days later we went to visit Trapper again. The dog had not moved. This time Ronda asked me if Trapper ever let the poor dog in the house. I had to tell her no. The dog was dead the first time that we came to visit. It was just a yard ornament now.

Alcohol had taken its toll on Trapper. His voice was raspy, and you could see that his all-around health was on a rapid decline. He was out drinking one night, and took someone's prescription drug. I heard that he died of an overdose, but I will never know for sure. I knew Trapper well enough to know that his abuse of alcohol alone would kill him someday. When I met Trapper, he was popular and well-liked by everyone. The last time I saw him was just weeks before his death. He was trying to be cool, but all I felt was pity. I had the chance to tell him one last story before he died, and I will tell you what I told him. When I was telling this story I had already quit drugs and alcohol, and I was going to church regularly.

I was working on my friend Dan's house with Hank. I fell down and a nail went in the palm of my hand. I also had tendinitis so bad in my hands that at night I would sit on the edge of my bed and cry. I was also being tempted to go see my old friends and party a little. That Wednesday evening at church when the pastor got ready to preach he stopped and said that the Lord told him that he wanted to bless someone. The person that he wanted to bless fell down and had a hole in the palm of his hand. Fuzz got excited and he tried to get me to go up front and tell the pastor that it was me. No way, I was not going up there; besides, that could be anybody.

Then the pastor said that the Lord must really want to bless this person because He just told him that the person that He wanted to bless had tendinitis in their hands so bad that every night they sat on their bed and cried. I still would not go up there. The pastor waited a minute and said that he could not wait any longer. He had to start the service.

Just as he was about to start, the Lord told him that the person that he wanted to bless was also being tempted to go back to their old lifestyle and party again. Christians call that backsliding. That was three in a row. That was enough for me. I went forward and God touched me. I had been praying for weeks that God would teach me to love Him, and He answered my prayer.

I don't know if Trapper believed this story or not. All I know is that God used me to try to reach Trapper.

Don't let me forget about Hank. Hank lived with his grandmother most of his childhood years. She was a strong Christian woman, and Hank was going to get a Christian upbringing, his Grandmother would make sure of that. Hank was going to be raised in a Christian home like it or not. When Hank was a teenager His friends made their own homemade crank. They would inject the drug to get high. Hank would even use a needle to inject his prescription drugs even if they were supposed to be taken orally. Hank had family members convinced that he had quit doing drugs so when he died they thought it was from a natural death. It was not. Friends of mine were there with him the night that he died.

My faith in the Lord was obvious to all of my friends. Even though I was a drug addicted, alcohol drinking, womanizing, dead beat dad, I still witness to all of my friends. They all knew that I believed in God. Most of them knew that deep down I was miserable. Some of them even knew why. The Bible says in **Matthew 6:24**"No one can serve **two masters**; for either he will hate the one and love the other, or he will be devoted to one and despise the other. You cannot serve God and wealth."

My whole life I was trying to serve two masters, and I was miserable. I do not know if I ever reached anybody with my faith in Jesus. I only know that I was in the car with Rummy when he died. I had the chance to tell Leo about Jesus before he was murdered, but I did not. I had a very unusual visit from Butch before he murdered his girlfriend, and it was my one chance to tell him about Jesus. I stayed silent. I went to jail three times, and each time I asked God to forgive me and I promised Him that I would change. I did not.

Red and I could have killed Fred when he was our fuel pump but we did not care. Walt committed suicide, but I was not there. Brian lost both of his legs. Should I have taken his keys? My brother was stabbed in the lungs and almost died. Was that my fault? My two nieces died and I was not there for the family of either one of them. My friend Joe lost his sobriety, and then he lost his life just hours after leaving my house. Could I have prevented his accident?

Pattie got killed in a car wreck and died after she left my house; Sam murdered his wife while he was drinking, but I was not there. Ralph's sister committed suicide, and I never told him about Jesus. Steve got killed in an accident while racing me, but that could not be my fault, could it? And what was I supposed to do when I saw the teenage kids partying with the wild bunch? Was there anything that I could do?

I was nowhere near Tonya, Chip or Brenda when they killed themselves so you can't blame me. My friend Hank told me that he thought that he was going to die from drugs just months before he did. Was he looking for help? Then there was Trapper, I told him about Jesus many times, but would you have listened to me knowing how I was living?

All of these people in this book were in a Spiritual battle along with me. I should have said more about Jesus to them than I did. I cannot change the past but, hopefully, God will use what I am saying in this book to help you change your future.

Printed in the United States
By Bookmasters